11311

Date Rape &

Acquaintance

Rape

Andrea Parrot, Ph.D.

THE ROSEN PUBLISHING GROUP, INC./ NEW YORK

Published in 1988 by The Rosen Publishing Group, Inc.
29 East 21st Street, New York, NY 10010

First Edition

Parrot, Andrea.
    Coping with date rape & acquaintance rape / Andrea Parrot. — 1st ed.
        p.   cm.
    Bibliography: p.
    Includes index.
    ISBN 0-8239-0784-8: $12.95.   ISBN 0-8239-0808-9 (pbk.): $7.95
    1. Rape—United States—Prevention.   2. Dating (Social customs)
3. Sexual ethics.   4. Youth—United States—Sexual behavior.
5. Rape victims—Services for—United States.   I. Title.
II. Title: Coping with date rape and acquaintance rape.   III. Title:
Date rape.
HV6561.P37   1988
362.8'8—dc19   88-1873
                                                                      CIP

Manufactured in the United States of America

ABOUT THE AUTHOR ◇

Dr. Andrea Parrot, a member of the faculty of Cornell University, focuses her professional work on acquaintance rape prevention and human sexuality. At Cornell she teaches a course on Human Sexuality and Social Policy. She is also a Clinical Assistant Professor of Psychiatry at the SUNY Health Sciences Center of Syracuse, New York, where she teaches a medical school course on Sexuality. She also teaches a women's self-defense course and several graduate courses.

A 1980 Cornell University Edward Sheldon Scholar, she has been a consultant to numerous colleges, universities, educational media producers, federal and state agencies, and crime prevention programs. She was awarded the 1987 Distinguished Teaching Award at Cornell. Dr. Parrot is a long-standing member of the Education Committee of Planned Parenthood of Tompkins County, New York, and was a founding member of the Cornell University Sexual Assault Prevention Coalition. Her manual *Acquaintance Rape and Sexual Assault Prevention* is viewed as a leading work in the field and has been recommended by *MS.* magazine.

Acknowledgments

A book on acquaintance rape is difficult to write because many people don't understand the issue, and many don't want to. That may be because once we confront the reality of acquaintance rape we must confront the possibility that we may have been or will be involved in it. Therefore it is important to present the information in such a way that people can hear it without being frightened or turned off.

Several people were very valuable to me in this effort. All of those who gave me feedback and comments on the manuscript had special expertise as victims, educators, professionals working with the issue, or as teenagers interested in making the world safer for themselves and others. Three who provided tremendous insights and understanding were Stephen V. Allen, Jr., M.D., Carol Bohmer, J.D., Ph.D., and Rosalind Kenworthy, M.S. In addition, I owe thanks to Stephanie Lampert, Julie Allen, Renee Vargason, Janet Salmons-Rue, John Simon, and Daniel Allen for their patient comments and help in making the book appropriate for young people who have been or are at risk of being raped by acquaintances.

I am especially grateful to all the victims of date and acquaintance rape who agreed to be interviewed. They have shared their stories so that I could share them with you. All the case studies really happened, but some of the details have been changed so that the victims could not be identified.

Contents

Introduction

If you are reading this book you may have been the victim of date or acquaintance rape. If so, you have faced some difficult emotions. Few people around you understand what you are going through, or even that you have been raped. You may not even be sure exactly what happened to you, or who is to blame.

You are sure that something is wrong. Things are not the same as they used to be. Interpersonal relationships are strained—with peers, because you don't know whom you can trust, and with your family, because you don't know how they will react. You want to be able to tell someone and get help to make things the way they used to be, but you don't know how.

This book will help you with those concerns. You will learn how to cope with the aftermath of date or acquaintance rape, where you can go for help, what you can expect from others, and what you can do to prevent your becoming a victim again.

The book is not for females only. Males may also be victims of date or acquaintance rape or sexual assault (the definition varies from state to state). If you are a male victim, you are not alone. Others have been through it before, and others can help you cope with your feelings and needs.

As a male, you may think that your "macho" behavior toward women is acceptable, even if you have pushed some young woman to have sex when she said no. Chapter

X will help you understand what that type of behavior means to the woman you "pushed." In addition, you will learn new ways of interacting with women so that you don't have to force them to have sex anymore.

This is a difficult issue to to cope with, but with the proper skills and understanding you can do it.

CHAPTER 1

"It Wasn't Rape, He Just Took Advantage of Me"

MELANIE

During her fourth week at college Melanie was asked out by a junior who was on the football team. She and all her friends knew that Kurt was one of the most popular and eligible men on campus. Melanie couldn't believe that Kurt would look at her, much less ask her for a date. They were lab partners in biology class and seemed to get along well when they were working together.

Kurt asked Melanie to a party after the first home football game. The party was wild, with lots of beer, loud music, roughhousing, and dancing. It was held at a house where many of the football players lived. Melanie and Kurt danced together between beers, and Melanie's seductive dancing drew stares of admiration from most of the men. She didn't notice this because she was rapidly becoming drunk. At one point there was a beer fight, during which almost everyone got wet to some degree, but Kurt and Melanie were drenched. Melanie was very uncomfortable in her wet and smelly clothes. She told Kurt that she had to go home and change. Besides, she was feeling a little uncomfortable about Kurt's kissing and fondling her in front of his friends. She excused his behavior on the ground that he was so drunk he didn't know what he was doing. She liked kissing him but not in front of his friends.

Kurt begged her to stay and said she could put on some of his clothes. He had a clean football jersey that was so large it would fit Melanie like a dress. He told her that there was a bathroom upstairs where she could clean up, and she could lock the door. It sounded like a good plan, and she really didn't want to leave. She was having a good time and she was worried that Kurt would take up with one of the other girls at the party, which might blow her chance to date him again.

After she had changed she met Kurt in his room, where she was going to leave her clothes. Sitting on the bed, he told her that she looked really foxy in that jersey and that she had nice legs. He walked over to her, kissed her, and closed the door. Then he picked her up and carried her over to the bed. She protested that she thought they should go back downstairs and get more beer, but Kurt produced a full pitcher and poured her a glass. Melanie was feeling uneasy, but she did not know how to get Kurt downstairs without sounding like a prude.

Kurt said that he had admired Melanie ever since he had first seen her and was very happy when they were assigned as biology lab partners. He told her that he really wanted to get to know her better. She said that she did too and that they should spend more time together. She asked him who his favorite rock star was. He said Madonna because she was sexy and reminded him of Melanie. Then he said, "Let's see how well you move to this song," and he put on "Like a Virgin."

Kurt pulled the jersey up and tried to fondle and kiss Melanie's breasts. She was feeling really good, but she didn't think that they should be doing anything more than that on the first date. She was afraid that Kurt wouldn't want to stop if they went any further. She decided that they could touch above the waist but nothing more, so they continued that for a while. When Kurt started to remove her underpants she protested vigorously and said that she didn't want to at that time. Kurt got angry and called her a tease. He said he knew she "wanted it" by the way she had danced and responded to his advances. She had danced like Madonna downstairs and had been giving him sexual come-ons all night. She was not going to stop him now.

Kurt, who weighed 230 pounds, got on top of Melanie (who weighed 110) and forced her to have sexual intercourse until he came (ejaculated). Then he passed out on top of her. She could not move until he rolled over about half an hour later. She got up, put on her wet clothes, and went home.

Would you consider this rape? Many people would not, perhaps not even Melanie. She may tell her friends that

Kurt took advantage of her, or she may not tell anyone at all. Melanie was a virgin before Kurt forced her to have sex, and she feels terrible about the whole event.

Melanie is likely to blame herself for what happened. She doesn't know how to feel or what to think. She is very confused because she thinks she may have been responsible. After all, she did go to his room voluntarily, was dancing very suggestively, was drunk, and she did let Kurt partially undress her and fool around with her. Maybe she was leading him on or teasing him. She shouldn't have gone back to his room, shouldn't have gotten drunk, and shouldn't have let him undress her, but she did. She didn't yell and scream, didn't fight, was not bruised or beaten. Because of all that very few people would consider this rape. But it was rape!

Melanie was the victim of a typical acquaintance rape. Unfortunately, many people experience acquaintance rape. It is far more common than stranger rape, yet we don't hear about it nearly as often. That is because most people think that in rape the attacker is a total stranger who jumps out of the bushes; the victim is beaten; is young, attractive, financially well off, and is hysterical. Some of those factors are present in stranger rape situations, but fewer of them are present in acquaintance rape. So, because victims of acquaintance rape do not have the commonly accepted rape experiences, most people are more likely to believe the victim of stranger rape than acquaintance rape.

Myths About Acquaintance or Date Rape

Myth: A rapist is always a stranger.

Fact: Most rape happens between two people who know each other. For example, they may be dating, friends, family friends, classmates, or fellow workers. Most acquaintance rape happens in his or her home. The Federal Bureau of Investigation has estimated that fewer than one in ten rapes are reported to the police, but most of the reported rapes are stranger rapes. Several studies made at colleges and universities indicate that fewer than one in 100 acquaintance rapes are reported to the police.

Myth: Women are always the victims.

Fact: Both men and women can be victims of rape. Some state laws define rape as something that only a man can do to a women, but in other states both women and men can be legally considered victims or assailants. Men are victims in approximately 10 percent of all sexual assaults, but men are less likely than women to report being raped. Many men are embarrassed and feel others will make fun of them or not believe them. They think men are supposed to be always ready and willing for sex with women. Men are also victimized by men. They may not report the assault because they they are embarrassed or fear others will think they are homosexual. In fact, rape is violence expressed in a sexual way, but to the victim it is very different from consensual sex.

Because victims are usually women and assailants are most often men, that terminology is used in the rest of the book. However, the reverse could be true in any of the situations discussed. Similarly, the situations could occur in homosexual relationships as well as heterosexual relationships. Often, the interaction between male and female sex roles contributes to acquaintance rape. For that reason acquaintance rape is primarily a heterosexual rather than homosexual phenomenon.

Myth: A woman is truly a rape victim if she is hysterical and bruised.

Fact: Immediately after a rape the victim may be in shock or may be hysterical. Shock is the more common response. The victim is likely to appear calm and collected but is actually suffering from rape trauma syndrome. This is an emotional disorder that requires prompt medical attention. It is discussed in detail in Chapter IV.

Most victims of date or acquaintance rape are not bruised, cut, or beaten. The victim often thinks the assailant will come to his senses at any moment. After all, he is a nice guy and wouldn't force her to do anything. She may know him well enough to know that he becomes violent when drunk or angry and therefore be afraid to fight. She may not want to embarrass him or herself by screaming because she is sure he will stop when he realizes what he is doing. She can't believe that anyone who likes her would rape her, and since she thinks he likes her, she thinks he will stop.

Myth: Rape victims are young, attractive, financially well off, and white.

Fact: Any woman can be a victim of rape, and any man can be a victim of sexual assault. Rape happens to women of all social classes, of all ages and occupations. Even prostitutes can be raped, although some believe that if a woman has had sex with hundreds of men she has given up her right to say no.

Many people believe that nobody would willingly have sex with an unattractive woman or an older woman, and that such women would be willing to have sex with anyone. Similarly, minority and poor women are often rape victims, but they are believed less often than white women or well-to-do women. This train of thought implies that rapists select only women who are sexually attractive, that unattractive women must have "wanted it" and purposely allowed it to happen. That is not true.

Most people don't believe that a man can be the victim of acquaintance rape or sexual assault by a woman because men are supposed to be always ready and willing to have heterosexual sex. If a man is forced by another man many believe that he should be strong enough to fight off his attacker. In reality, men are forced to have sex by men and women, but very few ever report the rape.

Types of Rape

Most date rapes occur because a man has planned to have sex. In other words, the man probably did not plan at the start of the evening to rape the woman, but he did intend to have sexual intercourse with her. Sex would be the perfect end to the evening for him. He may know that his buddies will want a report from him about his sexual experiences the previous night, and he wants to have something to tell them. In addition, he may have been fantasizing about a sexual end to the evening ever since he made the date.

JAN

John believed that Jan had sex with everyone she dated (even if the reputation was unfounded) and so he "knew" that she would have sex with him. Since Jan asked John out, he thought that meant she was "easy" and "loose" and really wanted to have sex with him.

When Jan said no to sexual intercourse at the end of the date, John felt teased, tricked, and disappointed. He felt that he had a right to sex, especially because he spent a lot of money for dinner. He interpreted Jan's nonverbal signals as indicating that she wanted to have sex too. She had gone to his apartment, and they had kissed and "fooled around" (fondling breasts and genitals), and they were both sexually aroused.

Not all men would rape given these circumstances. Many men stop if the woman says no but are frustrated and angry because they didn't get what they wanted. Just because a man is frustrated and angry does not necessarily mean that he will rape.

Planned Sex That Turns to Rape

In date rape situations the man has been planning sex, premeditating sex. If the woman turns him down he may become angry and do what he feels he has to do to get what he wants and thinks he deserves. A man is much more likely to push his date to have sex if he has been drinking. All other factors being equal, the degree of the man's intoxication is the best predictor as to whether acquaintance rape will occur.

Definitions of rape vary by state. In some states rape is defined as penile/vaginal contact; in others all forms of forced sex are considered rape (such as forced oral sex, forced anal sex, and forcing of objects into sexual orifices). Marital status is also a determining factor in rape law in some states. In about half of the states a woman may not charge her husband or live-in boyfriend with rape. The definitions that follow are general regarding the above factors but outline the differences among acquaintance rape, date rape, marital rape, and soft rape.

The meaning of the term *force* may include physical force, threat of force, violence, threat of violence, coercion, or threat of coercion. In most states if a victim is fearful for her life or her safety and has sexual intercourse (penetration of penis into vagina) under those circumstances, it is legally considered rape. For example, if a victim has sex because an assailant implies that he has a weapon and is willing to use it, the situation is legally defined as rape even if the assailant does not have a weapon.

Acquaintance rape is forced sexual intercourse (or other sexual act) that occurs between two people who know each other. The relationship can be any acquaintanceship, including a date, teacher/student, friend of the family, friend, employer/employee, husband/wife, doctor/patient. Date rape is only one form of acquaintance rape.

Date rape is forced sexual intercourse (or other sexual act) that occurs between a dating couple or while on a date.

Marital rape is forced sexual intercourse (or other sexual act) that occurs between husband and wife. Some states do not legally recognize this as rape. Even in states where marital rape is against the law, it is almost impossible to obtain a conviction unless the couple are separated or divorced, or unless some other form of violence such as assault and battery accompanies the rape.

Soft rape is forced sexual intercourse (or other sexual act) in which coercion (pressure or intimidation) or threat of coercion is used to gain the victim's compliance.

JANET

Janet and Bill were driving in his car at 1:00 a.m. in an isolated woods about ten miles from the nearest town. Bill told Janet that he wanted to show her his favorite spot to "commune with nature." It was winter, very cold, and snowing. Bill said he liked this spot best with a new snowfall, because it was so pure and clean.

Janet had completely lost her bearings on the way

to the woods. When Bill stopped the car and started to make sexual advances, Janet tried to stop him. Bill said, "The last girl I was with didn't want to have sex with me, so I let her out right here." Janet knew she would never find her way back before she froze. She also thought that the proverbial stranger rapist might be lurking behind a tree out there in the dark. She had sex with Bill without further protest.

This was soft rape because Janet was fearful for her life and her safety. Bill did not coerce her, but he threatened coercion. Even if most people would have been able to find their way out of the woods and back to safety, if Janet could not or believed she could not, the situation was rape. Janet was coerced because of her fear and lack of survival skills. The way others would have reacted has no bearing on Janet's situation, because no one else was there to help Janet. However, others who listen to Janet's story (such as family, friends, police, district attorney) may tell her it was not rape and blame her, saying that they would have been able to find their way out of the woods or that she shouldn't have let him take her there. Regardless of the ability of others, Janet did not feel capable of finding her way out of the woods in safety.

Stranger Rape

In contrast to acquaintance rape, which is usually a planned attempt to have consensual sex, stranger rape is premeditated rape. Stranger rape usually begins in the mind of the rapist as an attempt to degrade and overpower the victim. Some stranger rape occurs incidentally in connection with another crime; for example, when someone breaks into a house to burglarize but decides to rape the woman who is home. In acquaintance rape it is sex that is planned, rather than a crime. In acquaintance rape, if sex does not happen as planned, then rape occurs in which the assailant overpowers the victim to get what he wants, sex. He may want to degrade the victim as well.

Types of Rapists

Nicholas Groth, author of *Men Who Rape*, describes three types of rapists; the power rapist, the anger rapist, and the sadistic rapist. The power rapist rapes to feel powerful. He exerts as much power as needed to rape his victim. If the victim does not resist, very little power is used. If the victim does resist, the rapist exerts as much power as necessary to be successful, so the victim may be bruised. Most acquaintance rapes are power rapes, and because most victims do not fight back, they rarely have external bruises or cuts.

The anger rapist is angry at women in general or at a particular woman. If the victim reminds him of that woman, he is likely to be more violent. It would be a mistake for a victim to use the strategem of saying, "Think how you would feel if someone did this to your mother"; he might be raping because he was angry at his mother. Victims usually experience even more violence at the hands of the anger rapist than the power rapist.

The sadistic rapist has an urge to torture and mutilate. This type comprises a very small percentage of all rapists, but he is the most dangerous. He will probably rape, torture, mutilate, and kill his victim. The victim of a sadistic rapist should fight back and try to escape no matter how much force the rapist exerts, because the probable alternative is an excruciatingly painful death. It is difficult to know which type a rapist is, but if he is violent from the start you may do best to try to escape even if you have to be violent.

Acquaintance rapists rarely fall into the last two categories. Most acquaintance rapes are power rapes, and a power rapist will exert as much force as necessary to overpower his victim. Fighting with a power rapist may result in physical injury.

If a potential acquaintance rape victim thinks her best choice is to try to prevent the rape by self-defense, she should wait until the assailant has let down his guard to escape or to execute a self-defense technique to a sensitive target area. Unfortunately, most women do not know how to perform an effective technique or what constitutes a sensitive target area. A course in self-defense may provide those skills. A woman usually has the element of surprise on her side if she decides to employ self-defense because the assailant is not likely to expect her to know how.

The best strategy against acquaintance rape is to avoid it by keeping out of vulnerable situations. A woman can do this by evaluating the risks in her environment and by carefully reading verbal and nonverbal cues from her companion. She should make sure in advance that she has a ride home from a party with friends. By having enough money for a cab she can avoid having to ask her date to drive her home. Since most acquaintance rapes occur in the man's or the woman's home, dorm room, or apartment, it is best not to go with a date alone to any of those places. Melanie increased her risk of becoming a victim of acquaintance rape by going to Kurt's room. Almost all acquaintance rapes follow a specific pattern. It is important for girls and women to know this pattern and try to interrupt it.

Patterns in Acquaintance Rape

Researchers Groth and Birnbaum identified a three-stage behavior pattern in acquaintance rapes. First, a rapist does something to make a woman feel uncomfortable (for instance, putting his hand on her knee or kissing her in public after knowing her for just a few hours). This is common in fraternity party and bar situations when the music is so loud that the couple must be very close to hear each other.

If the victim does not clearly object, the rapist proceeds to the second stage in which he desensitizes the victim to the intrusion by escalating the behavior (moving his hand to her buttocks, for example). She may feel uneasy at this behavior and suggest going outside for "fresh air." The real reason behind her suggestion is to avoid letting her friends see how forward he is being, or to keep him from being so close to her. Unless she actually tells him that she is uncomfortable with his "roaming hands," he may misinterpret her suggestion as meaning that she wants to be alone with him. The third stage occurs when they are in an isolated place and the rapist insists on intercourse.

The use of alcohol and drugs is often related to incidents of acquaintance rape. Peer group expectations usually include consumption of alcohol at social events. Alcohol reduces inhibitions and dulls perceptions so that the woman is less likely to be alert and the man is less concerned about the needs of his date. In addition, if alcohol is involved in situations where peer pressure is brought to bear on normally moral men, they are more likely to behave in an immoral way. For example, they may participate in a gang rape while under the influence of alcohol, whereas they would condemn such behavior when sober. A woman who avoids or minimizes alcohol consumption is better able to avoid acquaintance rape. She also needs to be acutely aware of her date's alcohol or drug use and to leave the scene if he is "high."

CHAPTER 2

You Are Not Alone

Although exact figures are not available, we can make a fair estimate of the number of stranger or acquaintance rapes in this country each year. The FBI reports that about 82,000 rapes are reported to the police each year in the United States. Those are primarily stranger rapes. It is believed that acquaintance rapes are much more frequent. A survey of college women indicated that they had experienced acquaintance rape much more often than stranger rape, but they were more likely to report the stranger rape to the police.

It is not known what percentage of rapes are reported. Those that are reported are like the tip of an iceberg; we don't know how much of the iceberg is below the surface of the water. If only one tenth of rapes are reported (a conservative estimate), that would mean that almost 1 million rapes occur in the United States each year. However, several researchers have reported that less than one out of 100 acquaintance rapes are reported to law enforcement authorities. That makes rape a highly significant problem that will affect approximately one in four women during their lifetime.

Although any woman is a potential victim of stranger or acquaintance rape, certain types of women are more likely to become victims, while others are better able to prevent rape. That does not mean that there is a set of tried and true methods to keep a woman safe from rape, but there are things women can do to make themselves less vulnerable. In any case, however, a woman does not cause her rape. The person who rapes is the one responsible for it.

Who Is at Risk?

Rapists are more likely to select victims who do not appear strong, assertive, and able to take care of themselves. Certain characteristics are more common in victims than in nonvictims. These characteristics include personality elements such as being unassertive or having low self-esteem. Some women are more vulnerable because they live in cities where crime is more common, or because they go out on dates often.

Females as Victims

Research has shown that women with low self-esteem are more likely to be victims of rape. Other factors are traditional female behaviors determined by sex-role stereotypes, such as a woman's desire be popular in her peer group, her feeling that she doesn't control her own environment, and the absence of emotional help following victimization. That does not mean that that every woman who possesses these traits will become an acquaintance rape victim, nor that those who don't have these traits are immune.

Nor is it your fault if you have these traits and you are raped. It is never a victim's fault when a crime is committed against him or her. Some people think that if only they had changed they would not have become a victim and they go on to the still more erroneous conclusion that the rape was therefore their fault.

Low Self-Esteem. If you don't feel good about yourself you may feel that your needs are not as important as the needs of others. That is not true, but if you believe it is, you may not feel able to ask for what you want. Have you ever been in a situation in which someone asked you what movie you wanted to see and you said, "I don't care" when you really did care? You may have said that because you thought the other person wanted to see something else and you didn't want to interfere with his fun.

If you have been in situations in which you don't ask others to stop doing something that you don't like, such as blowing cigarette smoke in your face, it may be because you have low self-esteem and you don't think your needs are as important as someone else's. Chapter VIII contains suggestions on how you can work on improving your self-esteem.

Communication. The feelings that keep you from insisting on your rights may also keep you from asking a man to stop doing sexual things to you if you don't like them. If he forces you to have sex, it is acquaintance rape. But if you do not clearly let him know that you don't want to have sex with him, how can he know? It is important to make your wishes known if you expect your partner to honor them.

Sex-Role Stereotypes. Young women who believe that the best way for them to interact with men is to be a traditionally stereotyped female (gentle, kind, subtle, sacrificing, flirtatious, and manipulative) are more likely to be raped than assertive young women. Traditional female stereotypes prevent women from being direct and stating or asking for what they want. Many traditional women often try to get what they want by manipulating another person, rather than being direct. Let's look at an example of how these behaviors may lead to acquaintance rape.

JANE

Jane prided herself on being a "perfect lady," so when Jim finally asked her out she was delighted. She had been wanting to date him for months, but he had not asked her, so she had to figure a way to get him to make the first move. She had her friend Emily tell Jim how wonderful Jane was and that she had just broken up with her boyfriend. Jim finally took the hint and asked Jane if she would like to go to the school football game.

At the game they sat with some of his friends, who had brought beer. The more they drank the louder they got. Jane did not like to drink, but she took a beer at the start of the game to be a "good sport." Jim's friends started insisting that Jane have more beer so she could really "enjoy the game," and they popped beer cans in her direction to spray her with beer. Jane didn't think it was funny but she didn't want to be a "stick in the mud" so she didn't say anything to Jim.

After the game Jim suggested that they go out for a hamburger, and Jane agreed, to get away from his friends. When he asked where she wanted to go, she said she didn't care, anything was all right with her. So he took her to his house. In the kitchen Jim told Jane where everything was, and he went into the living room to put on some music. Jane cooked dinner for the two of them and set the table with candles to make it look more romantic.

After dinner he started kissing her. She really enjoyed being close to him, with the music playing and in the candlelight. He began to push her to do sexual things she didn't want to do, and she tried to stop him by saying that she would like a beer. He got them each another beer and came back to continue where he left off. She didn't know what else to try, so she said she wasn't feeling well. He told her to relax, that sex would make her feel better. Finally she told him she wanted him to stop and he got angry. Jim said that she had been giving him the come-on all day (drinking at the game, telling him she wanted to go out alone with him, agreeing to go to his house, candlelight, asking for more beer). Who did she think she was now telling him to stop?

Jane was very confused. All she thought she did was to try to please him without complaining about his rowdy friends and their drinking. She would have preferred to go out for dinner, but she didn't want to seem pushy.

What if he forced her to have sex because he felt it was his right after she had "led him on"? He would have committed rape. But it is also true that Jane's behavior contributed to the confusion of the situation. Jane could have refused the beer during the game, told Jim's friends to stop spraying her with beer, or asked Jim to move with her. She could have insisted on going out for dinner. She could have told Jim earlier in their sexual encounter that she was feeling uncomfortable or just how far she was willing to go sexually. Unfortunately, all the things that Jane could have done did not seem traditionally feminine to her. A "lady," in her view, would not do those things.

Social Status. Imagine that Jim is very popular and Jane

almost never dates because she is unpopular. She may put up with things she doesn't like because she is afraid to lose him. This may feel like her last chance. Her social status will improve greatly if she goes out with Jim, because his girlfriends are considered part of the "in" group. Is she really willing to throw her newfound status and popularity away because he wants her to go further sexually than she wants?

To answer that question we must go back to self-esteem. If Jane feels good enough about herself not to trade sex for popularity, she will probably risk losing Jim as a boyfriend and tell him to stop forcing her sexually. On the other hand, if having a popular boyfriend is of utmost importance to her she may be willing to compromise sexually to some degree to keep the relationship. But if Jim wants her to go further than she is willing to go, it is rape.

Environmental Factors. Jane did not control her environment to increase her safety. If she had wanted to increase the likelihood of being safe sexually, she would not have stayed with his rowdy drinking friends. She would not have gone to his house. With her temperament she may have felt that there was no possibility of the kind of environment that would have made her feel safe. After all, she would have had to ask for what she wanted, which was contrary to her stereotypic sex-role behavior patterns.

Repeat Victimization. If Jane had been a victim of sexual assault before, she may not have known any other way of acting in a sexual situation. The previous sexual assault could have been with another date or with a relative or family friend. If Jane has learned to relate to men as a sexual victim, she may not know how else she can act, or she may feel that she has no right to act any other way. If that is true, Jane needs to learn other patterns of personal interaction. Suggestions for how to do this and how to deal with the other issues that have contributed to Jane's becoming a victim are given in Chapter VIII.

Males as Victims

Many of the patterns Jane encountered that contributed to her vulnerability to rape are also present when men are victims of sexual assault. Some male victims have some of the same personality characteristics as female victims. Low self-esteem, wanting to be a member of a high status group, not feeling in control of the environment, and previous victimization may all be contributing factors to sexual assault. Again, it is important to remember that a victim is never responsible for the crime; the person who commits the crime is the person who is responsible for it. There are things men can do, however, to make themselves less vulnerable to acquaintance sexual assault by either male or female assailants, for example, being careful about alcohol consumption and about not being in an isolated place with someone more powerful than you are. These suggestions are discussed in detail in Chapter VIII.

People who commit acquaintance sexual assault and acquaintance rape often look for the "victim type," people who are not assertive, who don't feel good about themselves, and who have few friends.

Few men who are victimized sexually ever report the assault to the police or anyone else. They are often more embarrassed than female victims because they fear that being a victim of a man means that they are homosexual. They may fear ridicule if they have been forced to have sex with a woman, because they think that men should always be ready and willing to have sex. Finally, they often believe that since males are supposed to be strong and powerful, they cannot let anyone know that they have been overpowered. Chapter IX further discusses males involved in sexual assault and acquaintance rape situations.

Acquaintance Rape During the Teen Years

Most rape, and specifically most acquaintance rape, happens between the ages of fifteen and twenty-five. This is the time when young women are most likely to date and therefore are most vulnerable to date rape. Acquaintance rape is not limited to dating situations; it may be committed by friends of the family, employers, friends, past boyfriends, and even husbands.

Acquaintance rape can happen anytime but is most likely during the teen years. This is true partly because many young women lack practice in dealing with sexual encounters. As they grow older, they are more likely to have learned from experience. In addition, because teenagers have more social freedom than their mothers did, young women are facing pressures in dating situations that their mothers did not have to deal with at such early ages. A fifteen-year-old today may have to deal with the same kinds of pressure her mother faced at twenty with more experience and maturity.

There are also very few "rules" for young people to follow today regarding dating, relationships, and sex. Young people receive conflicting messages from parents, peers, media, and religion. It may be difficult for them to decide what to do sexually, where, and how to draw the line, and few reliable sources of such information are available to them. They struggle through their relationships hoping to do the right thing, without knowing what the right thing is or how to accomplish it.

This book is designed to provide teenagers with information on these questions. Several good general books on sexuality for teenagers can be found in the library. You may want to discuss these issues with an adult whom you trust and can talk to. Parents can be a good resource for some, but not all parents are comfortable or competent about matters of sex, and they are likely to have grown up in more restrictive social settings. Other adults who may be good resources for discussion are relatives, teachers, counselors, youth group leaders, religious representatives, or friends. But even discussion with an informed adult who is easy to talk to will not always protect you from sexual assault. Each situation is different and may require different strategies and skills.

Acquaintance Rape in Adulthood

Even adults who have a better understanding of how to prevent acquaintance or date rape may still become victims of sexual assault. Many of the factors present in teenage acquaintance rape may also be present in adult acquaintance rape.

VICKI

Vicki had been married to Bob for over twenty years and was happy in her role as wife and mother. Both of her children were away at college, and she found herself with little to do with her time and not much to talk about with Bob when he came home from work. Her life had been very busy with the children when they were at home, but she had not found anything satisfying to fill the void left by their absence.

Bob was a successful attorney who sometimes worked late hours preparing cases. At the office he fell in love with a bright new woman attorney. He came home one day and told Vicki that he wanted a divorce because he no longer found her interesting and attractive and had fallen in love with someone else.

Vicki was devastated. She believed she derived all her status from being married to a successful attorney. Now she would have no husband, she had no job skills, and she worried that she could not compete with all the young women out there in the singles scene. But the thought of spending the rest of her life alone was more than she could bear. Vicki had not dated for twenty-five years, and she didn't think she would know how to play the "dating game," nor was she sure that she wanted to. She was hurt, rejected, discouraged, lonely, and angry.

Even though she was nervous and worried about dating, and she felt terrible about herself, she decided she had to go out and meet someone so she could begin to feel better. Vicki dated the first man who asked her out, an executive named Michael. She was unsure how she should act, but because he seemed a perfect gentleman she figured he would not do anything he shouldn't.

Michael figured that Vicki should be happy to go out with him, and he was looking forward to a great evening ending up in bed. Vicki did not have the same ending in mind, but since she and Michael never discussed the subject they were not aware of each other's expectations. Michael assumed that because Vicki had been married, sex would not be a "big deal." He assumed that she had had sex many times in the past, with Bob and others. "After all, isn't that the reputation divorced women have?", he thought.

They went out to dinner and then to Michael's

penthouse apartment for a nightcap. Michael insisted on sex, Vicki protested. Michael assumed that she was just playing hard to get, so he pushed her to have sex, assuming that she would thank him the next day.

Vicki felt even worse the next day. She felt that she had been raped, and she had.

Being older does not create immunity to acquaintance rape. Nor does age automatically give the understanding needed to be effective at avoiding acquaintance rape.

Some of the same factors that make young people vulnerable also increase vulnerability for older people. It was a bad time for Vicki because she was having trouble dealing with her emotions after the divorce. She had low self-esteem and felt that she needed to be involved with an important man to be important herself. She was unassertive and traditionally female in her behavior. All those factors increased her vulnerability, though they do not mean that she in any way caused the rape. She may be more effective in preventing rape in the future if she can understand how these factors make her vulnerable and if she works to decrease them.

Conclusion

It is important to consider rape a community problem. Society as a whole suffers from rape, acquaintance or stranger, violent or not. Women can become frightened of men and afraid of having relationships with them, and men can become worried for the women in their lives. This leads to untrusting relationships. Those who have been raped and their families suffer from emotional trauma that may interfere with their lives for years. And those who rape may think that it is acceptable to violate others.

Rapists tend to choose people who they think will be easy victims. Therefore, even if 99 percent of the possible victims are trained in rape prevention strategies, rape will still not stop because the remaining one percent will still be vulnerable. Therefore major prevention efforts should be where they belong, on men to stop raping. But as long as men attempt rape, we all will decrease our vulnerability as victims if we understand what makes a person a likely target for rape.

It is also very important that we do not assume that once we adopt the suggestions in this book we are invulnerable to rape. Rape can happen to anyone at any time. Rape prevention strategies help to decrease the risk, but the risk never drops to zero percent. Awareness prevention strategies are also very important for potential assailants, so that they know what constitutes rape.

CHAPTER 3

Why Does it Happen?—Sugar and Spice and Everything Nice

No one reason explains acquaintance rape. Unlike stranger rape, most acquaintance rape is not premeditated for the purpose of doing violence to a woman and degrading her. Stranger rape is premeditated *rape*. Acquaintance rape usually begins as premeditated or planned *sex* and ends in aggression only if the victim does not comply with the rapist's desire for sex. What is it about our culture that allows some persons to feel it is acceptable to force their wishes on others?

Forcing someone to have sex is an act of aggression (demanding your wishes without regard for the rights of others) rather than assertiveness (asking for your wishes without violating the rights of others).

Socialization

Neither boys nor girls are taught to be assertive in our culture. Boys are taught to be aggressive and to achieve their goals, often no matter what the cost. Girls are taught to be passive and to put the needs of others before their own. These behavior patterns set up the dynamic for acquaintance rape. For example, if Greg thinks it is manly to have sex on the first date, and Rebecca thinks it is feminine to flirt with Greg and tease him, Greg may rape Rebecca because he thinks he should have sex and because he thinks Rebecca wants it. The messages that contribute to this socialization pattern come from families, friends, school, books, television, movies, music; in short, from all around us.

Female Socialization

Little girls receive messages from the time they are born to act in a certain way. "Ladylike" behavior is quiet, passive, friendly, nonthreatening, pleasant, giving, caring, generous, neat, gentle, and nonviolent. Girls are taught to concede in arguments and act like the adult women around them. Any child who learned to read by being introduced to Dick, Jane, Sally, Spot, Puff, Mom, and Dad (the characters in the traditional first grade reader) learned that girls are supposed to cook for, serve, and clean up after boys while the boys sit at the table and are waited on. The messages we received from those readers confirmed what we observed around us: that females are supposed to do things for males and attend to their creature comforts.

Girls see as their role models adult women primarily in service occupations such as teaching, nursing, child care, social work, and secretarial work. These career choices reinforce the belief that women should serve others. In addition, these professions pay much less money than most "traditional" male occupations. Most Americans do not believe that "women's work" is as important as men's; therefore, women are not considered as important as men. In some families the boy is expected to grow up and carry on the family business, but there is no similar expectation for his sister.

The difference between the way boys and girls are treated even extends to the monetary value placed on their lives; for example, a life insurance policy is purchased for a son, but less insurance or none is purchased for the daughter. One of the acquaintance rape victims interviewed for this book explained that her parents bought life insurance for her brother because he was going to take over the family business. They did not buy any for her because she was "just going to get married." She felt much less important than her brother because of that.

These traditional attitudes are changing slowly, but many young men and women still believe that the sexes should behave in traditionally stereotyped ways. Because men and women of all ages go out on dates, these traditional views may be present in many dating situations.

All of these messages and hundreds of others like them reinforce the idea that boys are more important than girls. In addition, many people think that the only way a girl can really be successful in life is to marry and have a family, even if she has a successful career. Boys can be successful if they do well with their career, regardless of their marital status. Often a woman's success is measured by her association with a man, especially a successful man. The reverse is hardly ever true.

Young girls are not encouraged to play roughly or to experience physical trauma as boys are. Thus girls do not learn the message that it is not the end of the world to be knocked down, or to have the wind knocked out of you, or to experience pain or a black eye after a fistfight. If girls had had the experience that they could encounter physical injury and still function, more girls and women might fight back rather than submit to an attacker. By protecting girls from physical activity that may result in pain, we are encouraging them to be victims rather than fighters.

Girls are more likely to be encouraged by their parents to take dance and gymnastics rather than football and hockey. The traditional female activities do not provide the opportunity to learn how much violent contact one's body can take and still function. Nor do they provide the opportunity for a girl to learn that she is unlikely to incapacitate someone if she deals her hardest blow. If she doesn't know what target points are most vulnerable, even a properly executed self-defense technique will probably not allow her to get away. Many girls say that they could not hit another person for fear of hurting someone. Girls need to know that it is acceptable to hurt a person who is trying to hurt them. Studying martial arts would provide this type of information, but few girls take such training.

Even women who do learn martial arts are generally smaller and weaker than men. They may be able to minimize the power imbalance between men and women by learning self-defense, but the size and strength difference will always exist.

Male Socialization

A proud dad may buy a hockey stick or a football for an infant boy with the expectation that the boy will grow up and become a sports hero. The boy will encounter a number of physical injuries while learning these sports. He may even be praised for getting into a fight in a hockey game because that behavior is "manly." Contact sports develop physical strength and endurance, as well as giving young people some understanding of their physical limitations and pain threshold.

Boys also learn from the first grade reader that they are more important than girls. After all, Dick and Dad do active and interesting things, while Mom, Jane, and Sally prepare meals for them, serve the meals, and clean up after Dick and Dad. Based on real life experience, children learn that boys can grow up to be President of the United States; girls can't. Until Geraldine Ferraro in 1984, girls did not even have a chance at being Vice President. These are a few of the messages that set up a date rape dynamic. Some men believe that since they are more important they can do what they want (like force someone to have sex) at the expense of someone less important (like a girl) who doesn't want sex. Television, books, magazines, songs, newspapers continually reinforce the message that it is acceptable for men to force women to have sex.

Influence of the Media

Television is probably the most popular form of entertainment for young people today. Few current television shows provide responsible messages about sexuality. Programs such as "Family Ties," "The Cosby Show," "Designing Women." and "Diff'rent Strokes" are exceptions to the norm of portraying irresponsible sexual communication patterns. Many shows, however, portray women as not knowing what they want sexually or as manipulating others to get what they want. Rarely are women portrayed as being direct without also being "uppity" and "aggressive" and therefore undesirable. Television implies that women cannot be feminine and sexy as well as assertive and in charge of the situation.

Several years ago on the popular soap opera "General Hospital," Luke raped Laura. Her response was to marry him soon afterward. The message many people got from this situation was that the reason Laura didn't want to have sex with Luke was that she did not know how good he was in bed; once she experienced Luke's sexual expertise, she wanted to marry him so she could have constant access to such a "stud."

This type of message is not new. It was sent in the epic movie "Gone With the Wind" when Rhett Butler carried Scarlett O'Hara upstairs to the bedroom and raped her. The next morning she was delighted with herself and Rhett. Although the message is not new, it is dangerous, leading men to conclude that women don't know what they are missing and that if men just push them beyond their sexual limits women will be forever grateful.

This is the height of paternalism: men thinking they know what is best for women. Men are not the only ones who think this way. Some women also believe it, partly because they think that men know more about sex. If a man dictates how a sexual encounter should proceed, a woman may think he must be right and thus may have trouble believing in her own right to stop it.

Does No Ever Mean Yes?

Whether a woman who says no in a sexual relationship means it depends on the woman and the circumstance. Some women mean no the first time they say it; others don't mean no even after saying it many times. This variation makes it difficult for the woman who means no the first time she says it. Some men become desensitized to the word because so many of the women in their lives don't mean it. If a man persists in sexual advances after a woman has clearly said no, she may feel angry, frustrated, ignored, unimportant, and unheard. She may try to make him hear her or believe her by being more forceful physically (pushing him away). She may even scream, threaten him, try to escape, or to resort to physical violence (hitting him) to make her wishes understood. Why should all this be necessary if she clearly says no the first time and means it? Many women do know what they want in a sexual relationship but are treated as if they don't.

Many men are taught to believe that a woman never means what she says about anything, and they may be right in some instances. Girls and women are expected to be polite and not to say rude or hurtful things. For example, if a little girl were served chocolate pudding (which she usually loves) while having dinner at a friend's house, but the pudding tasted chalky, what would be her most likely response? "I don't want to finish this pudding because it doesn't taste good," or "I'm full, and I don't think I can eat any more right now." Or she may eat the pudding anyway. You probably chose the second response, which is a polite and typically female response. In that case, she is trying to get what she wants (not to eat the pudding) without being direct about her reason. The third response is the most polite of all, but one in which she gives up her rights completely.

Consider another common pattern: If a woman who is clearly distraught and upset is asked by an important man in her life, "What is wrong?" she is likely to respond, "Nothing." In reality something is wrong, and he knows it, especially if she is crying, but she tells him verbally that nothing is wrong. The message he receives from that inter-action is that he should pay attention to her body language and ignore her verbal message. After all, her verbal mes-sage told him that nothing was wrong; only her body lan-guage was consistent with his perceptions. What about women who say no when they really mean yes or maybe sexually? Some young men have told me that to them no means maybe and maybe means yes. When I ask how many times they have to hear no on a date before they believe it, the response ranges from "once" to "7,579."

Some men say that it depends on how she says no. For instance, if she says no and giggles, that implies yes. If she says no forcefully while removing his hand from her body, he may think she means it. But not all men would stop, especially if they think they know what is best for women or if they feel that sex is their right.

A woman who say no when she means yes runs the risk of "crying wolf," so that her partner may not believe her if and when she really means no. After all, she has been conditioning him all evening to disbelieve her verbal mes-sages. How will he know that all the earlier nos really meant yes but the most recent no meant no? Perhaps her accompanying body language should indicate to him that she really means what she says this time. And if he is con-siderate, reasonable, and views women as his equal, he may stop sexual advances at that point.

But what if Mike and Lori are on a special date. Mike has been fantasizing about this night for weeks, has paid $50 for dinner, and has been reading Lori's nonverbal messages as sexual come-ons. Even if Mike believes that Lori wants to stop, he may feel that he has a right to continue to push for what he wants. He may not be thinking clearly because he has drunk too much. He may be thinking that because he spent a lot of money, Lori owes him sex. He may think she is a tease; that she sent all those messages that she wanted sex too (going to his place for a "drink," saying she really wants to get to know him better) and now she has the nerve to change her mind. Although Mike thinks these behaviors mean Lori wants to have sex, he may be misinterpreting her nonverbal messages. Mike may have played out this date in his mind and for his buddies as hot, raw sex, and he thinks that anything less would make the evening a failure. Mike may force Lori to have sexual intercourse against her will, thinking that he has a right. He does not think of it as rape because to him rape is something committed by a stranger, in which violence is used, and after which the woman becomes hysterical.

Sexual Confusion

Lori may be unsure about what she really wants sexually, and so may Mike. Both of them have tapes playing in their minds from important people in their lives regarding what they should do sexually, but the two may be quite contradictory.

The message Lori got from her mother was probably, "Good girls don't," or "Don't you ever come home pregnant," or "It would kill your grandmother if she ever found out." Her father's message may have been something like, "I'll kill him." Girlfriends may say "Be careful!" or "It's O.K. if you really love the guy." Her boyfriend may say "Come on, everybody's doing it," or "You would if you really loved me." Religions give the message, "Wait until marriage," or "You should only have sex with the person you marry." The media messages are that "Sex is glamorous," and "Everybody is doing it."

Male messages are a little different because a double standard exists for men and women. Men are encouraged to have sex with many women before marriage to become sexually proficient. However, many men still want to marry innocent and sexually inexperienced women. Male messages usually sound more permissive than women's messages. Mother's tape may be, "I don't want to know about what you do." Father's tape may be, "Don't do anything I wouldn't do," or "Don't bring anyone home pregnant." Male peers' tapes include "Be a stud, go out and score, and have a good time," or "If you don't have sex something is wrong with you." Girlfriends may give mixed and confused messages such as, "I really want to, but I don't think we should."

As you can see, both males and females are receiving conflicting messages from many sources regarding sexual behavior. But young people also have their own ideas, which become confused with all the rest of the sexual messages. Young people may believe that they know what they want to do sexually before the date begins. Once on the date, however, in the "heat of passion," a decision of no intercourse may become increasingly difficult to stick with because of the deliciously sensual urges and desires that are normal in healthy people. When people become sexually excited, vaginal lubrication (wetness) in the female and erection in the male result from an involuntary rush of blood into the pelvic region. Since a larger than normal percentage of blood is in the pelvic region, blood is not rushing into the brain to help you make a good, well-reasoned decision. So even if one goes on a date with intentions of a nonsexual evening, his or her body may be contributing to conflicting feelings about sex.

Personifying the Penis

Some men use their view of their penis as an excuse to have sex. Have you ever heard the expression "The little head thinks for the big head"? It implies that the penis has a brain. Some people refer to a penis by a proper name other than that of the man it is attached to, for example, George, or Henry, or Horatio, or more recently in the movie *Peggy Sue Got Married* as "lucky Chuckie." Naming the penis personifies it. This is very dangerous because the man no longer takes responsibility for what the penis does; "Lucky Chuckie has a mind of his own and made me do it."

People often refer to the penis by other terms because they are uncomfortable using anatomical terms for body parts. Some of the terms are "cute," such as "weewee" or "dingaling"; others are angry, such as "ramrod"; others are polite, such as "private parts." All of these terms prevent us from discussing the concept of sexuality in an enlightened way. How can we help others understand facts or feelings about something if we refuse to identify clearly what we are talking about? For example, suppose you tried to say something about your elbow and you called it your "pointed joint"? Most people would think you were odd, and many would not know what you were talking about.

When my mother was young my grandfather used to refer to her genitals as her "china dishes." This is not a common term for the vagina, but it was understood in their home. Can you imagine what would have happened if my mother had gone on a date and said to her partner, "You can do anything you want as long as you don't touch my china dishes"? Using incorrect terms for body parts can contribute to the misunderstandings that lead to acquaintance or date rape.

Sexual Decision-making

To be able to make a good decision in a sexual situation, a person has to know how to make a good decision. Decision-making should be a process of careful reasoning about facts that leads to the best conclusion possible under the circumstances. Unfortunately, many of us make our sexual decisions by default; that is, what happens is the decision that was made for us, not the decision we made, and we are left to rationalize why the decision was a good one. Many of us are quite proficient at rationalizing, but that does not mean that the outcome was best for the situation.

JENNY

Jenny and Jordan, both sixteen, were on a date. Jenny had not thought carefully about whether she wanted to have sex with Jordan, or when she wanted to lose her virginity. They got drunk because they went to a party where alcohol was the only beverage being served. On the way home in the car Jordan pulled off the road to a secluded place and started making sexual advances. Jenny was too drunk to know what she was doing, but she had not passed out. Jordan had sex with Jenny, but without her consent because she was too drunk to give consent.

In this case, Jenny had sex by default. There had been no previous discussion about if, when, or under what circumstances they should have sex. If she had made a decision about sexual intercourse with Jordan, she would have considered many things: what they would use for contraception; what she would do if she became pregnant; how her family and friends would react; what if she contracted a sexually transmitted disease such as AIDS or gonorrhea; whether Jordan was the right person for her to lose her virginity with; the religious implications; the location of the event; how she would feel about herself and Jordan the next day; what would happen if he tried to force her. Jenny did not consider any of those things, but she did end up losing her virginity. If she was like most girls her age, she probably rationalized the event because she thought it meant Jordan loved her. She was "swept off her feet." The relationship is not likely to last, however. If Jordan does not agree that sex means love, he does not expect a long-term relationship with Jenny. After all, they are both young and have plenty of time to meet and date new people before they settle down.

In most states the situation between Jenny and Jordan would be considered rape, because Jenny, being drunk, was not able to consent. If a woman is under the influence of a substance (such as alcohol or drugs) that diminishes her reasoning ability, if she is asleep, mentally incompetent, or too young to understand what she is consenting to, under some state laws she is considered unable to consent; intercourse that take place under those circumstances is rape.

Attitudes About Forced Sex

Some men feel that in certain situations forced sex is permissible. Men's assumptions about their right to sex were studied in a survey at Texas A&M and Indiana Universities; 106 students were asked to respond anonymously regarding acceptability of behaviors in dating situations. Almost all the men felt that it was all right for a woman to ask a man out. They felt that he should accept the invitation but indicated that he might view the woman as very promiscuous.

The subjects were given three descriptions of dating interactions, which varied with respect to who initiated the date, where the couple went, and who paid. They were then asked if forced or coerced sex was justified in any circumstances. Men rated intercourse against the woman's wishes as significantly more justifiable when the woman initiated the date, when the man paid, and when the couple went to the man's apartment.

Thus we see that a woman's assertive actions as well as the passive behaviors discussed above may be interpreted by men as justification for rape. This does not necessarily mean that women should avoid assertive behavior with men, but rather that they should be aware of how assertiveness may be interpreted by some men.

Researchers at the University of California–Los Angeles asked similar questions of a group of teens. A large percentage (54%) of adolescent males responded that forced sex was acceptable if the woman said yes even though she later changed her mind. What if the woman said yes to kissing but no to intercourse? If she was not specific about what she was saying yes to, the man could interpret the yes to mean that sexual intercourse was acceptable.

Almost 40 percent felt that forced sex was acceptable if a man had spent a lot of money on a woman. This is the case in almost every dating situation. Men frequently feel that it is their responsibility to pay for the date, regardless of the cost, and regardless of who initiated the date. A good reason for a woman to pay her share is that the man is less likely to feel that he deserves sex. Over half of the men questioned believed that a man had a right to sex if she "led him on." But how can we define being "led on"? Is a woman "leading a man on" if she invites him out for a soda, or if she kisses him, or if she invites him to her house for coffee after a date, or if she accepts a drink he buys her in a bar? Do any of these things give him permission to force sex on her? He may think so if he believes such actions are intended to "lead him on."

Over one third of the men interviewed in the UCLA study believed that forced sex is acceptable if a man is so turned on that he thinks he can't stop. This is a myth about male sexuality. In fact there is no time in the male sexual response cycle, except for the split second before ejaculation, when he can't stop. He may not want to stop, or he may *feel* that he can't stop, but if his mother walked in on him during sexual arousal he almost certainly *would* stop. As a matter of fact, he probably would have trouble continuing. He may have heard about "blue balls," a phenomenon in which the testicles are engorged with blood as a result of prolonged sexual arousal without ejaculation. This phenomenon is uncomfortable, and he may have the idea that unless the pressure is relieved his testicles will explode, resulting in permanent sterility. Both boys and girls learn the myth about "blue balls," but in reality, of course, the testicles do not explode and the discomfort will not cause sterility. The discomfort dissipates quickly if the man ejaculates, or slowly if he does not. If a man does experience this discomfort, he does not have to have a female help him alleviate it. Rather than force his partner to have intercourse, he can masturbate, or he can allow the pressure to subside naturally over several hours. The distaste some people feel about masturbating is less of a problem than rape.

Solution to the Problem

Men must begin to understand that forced or coercive sex is rape even if the woman is a friend or a lover. There are many things men can do to see forced sex for what it is and to try to stop it on a personal or societal level. Chapter X deals in greater detail with the issue of male responsibility.

Since socialization is responsible for many of the attitudes that allow men to view forced or coercive sex as acceptable, socialization must be changed. Both men and women must be willing to explore the effects of traditional socialization in encouraging rape. College men can use peer pressure to condemn, rather than condone, the notion of women as conquests. When these men become adults they can have impact on the socialization of children. Men must try to educate others about the importance of viewing women as equals and of communicating clearly and consistently regarding feelings. Finally, men must know the facts about forced sex to avoid being arrested for rape when they thought they were "doing the woman a favor."

Women must understand the danger of "playing games" on dates, with no meaning maybe or yes. Women can make their lives safer if they understand the ways in which their behavior increases their vulnerability. If a woman is involved in socializing others, it is important for her to give responsible messages about sexual interaction patterns. Women can also use peer pressure to condemn irresponsible behavior exhibited by their friends. It is important to this and future generations that all of us try to change the traditional socialization patterns that contribute to a rape mentality.

CHAPTER 4

How Are You Feeling?

If you have been the victim of acquaintance or date rape you are probably experiencing many new and confusing feelings. You may be unsure what exactly happened to you and what it will mean to you. You may not even be sure whether it was your fault. Should you tell anyone? If so, whom should you tell? How will they react? Will they believe you? How are you feeling about yourself?

What does this mean about you? If you were forced to have sex but you did lead the guy on, whose fault is it? You may have invited him to your house after the date, or you may have gone to his. You may have been drinking, or you may have been drunk. What if you were wearing seductive clothing, such as a low-cut blouse or a skirt with a very high slit? Does that mean you were asking for it? THE ANSWER IS NO!

What he did to you was force his penis into your vagina. That is rape. In most states rape is sexual intercourse against a woman's will and without her consent. In other states other sexual encounters also constitute rape. In some states, any forced sexual encounter is considered rape, with either a man or a woman as victim. Even if you did go to his house or were drunk, if you did not give your consent or if you said no but sexual intercourse occurred, it was rape. Many people in these situations do not call what happened to them rape. They say that they got themselves into a bad situation, or they were taken advantage of. In fact, they were raped.

The Rape Trauma Syndrome

Most victims who have been sexually assaulted experience the rape trauma syndrome. This consists of a series of phases: the acute or crisis phase, the disorientation phase, and the reorientation phase. In the crisis phase, immediately following the rape, victims may be calm (in shock) or upset (angry or guilty), or inappropriately carefree. During this time many victims report feeling powerlessness, fear, anxiety, shame, embarrassment, shock, guilt, depression, and disbelief. This phase may last days or even longer.

In the disorientation phase victims are not sure how to act and may have trouble interacting with others. They may try to repress the memory of the rape. Sometimes they change their behavior patterns significantly to avoid future involvement. They may stop dating to avoid putting themselves in situations where they think acquaintance rape could occur. Since they are not sure why the rape did occur, they may stop doing almost anything outside of home. Fearful that the memory of the rape will be triggered by some event, they limit their activities and the number of people with whom they interact.

In the reorientation phase the victim is feeling stronger and has some idea of how and why the rape happened. She can begin making constructive changes in her life to regain some control and freedom. She realizes that she will never be able to go back to the way things were before the rape, but she can incorporate the rape into her life to make her future something positive. Counseling and the support of a friend or relative help most women to reach such an emotionally positive stage. Unfortunately, not all rape victims reach this phase. Some try to repress the memory and never get out of the disorientation phase.

What Does Being Raped Mean About You?

If you were a virgin before you were forced to have sex, are you still a virgin? What is virginity? Virginity can be defined physically (according to the absence or presence of the hymen, the skin covering the vaginal opening), or behaviorally (according to whether you have had sexual intercourse), or emotionally (based on your freely giving yourself sexually to someone else). The presence or absence of the hymen is not a good indicator of virginity. Some women are born without a hymen, and most lose the hymen in nonsexual activities such as riding a bicycle, gymnastics, inserting a tampon, or having a gynecological exam. In a small number of women the hymen must be surgically removed because it is solid and prevents passage of menstrual flow. Even though these women no longer have a hymen, they are clearly virgins if they have not had sexual intercourse.

Thus, we cannot define virginity by the presence or absence of the hymen, so we should consider it as a behavioral and emotional condition. If you have consensual sexual intercourse, you are not a virgin. But until you do, you still are.

If we define a virgin as a person who has not had sexual intercourse, we can still include victims of date or acquaintance rape in the category. A victim of rape did not have consensual sexual intercourse; she was a victim of sexual violence. That being the case, she is still a virgin.

Rape Does Not Make You "Easy"

Just because you have had nonconsensual sex once with someone, you are not obligated to have sex again with that person or anyone else. In fact, rape does not mean anything about you as a willing sexual partner because you did not decide to have sex. The decision was taken away from you.

Some victims of date rape react by believing that they do not have a right to say no to any other man. This is true especially of victims of date or acquaintance rape who were virgins at the time. These women may have believed that virginity is good, and nonvirginity is bad. Now they believe that they are nonvirgins and consequently are bad. They may think they no longer have the right to put their needs before the needs of others. Some women also believe that virginity is the only acceptable reason to refuse sexual intercourse. Once they no longer perceive themselves as a virgin, they feel they no longer have an acceptable reason to say no to sex.

In reality, any person has the right at any time to say no to any sexual act, regardless of how many times she or he has had sex before with any partner. She or he even has the right to say no to a previous consensual sex partner. This is a moral and legal right.

Being a Rape Victim Does Not Make You Bad

You may also feel that when you have been the victim of acquaintance or date rape you are bad because you have had sex before marriage, or that you have a "loose" reputation. Remember that you did not have consensual sex, and therefore you cannot be held accountable for that act of sexual intercourse.

Imagine that you were taking your final science exam. Without your consent the person next to you was cheating, copying your answers on his paper. This was something you were involved in, but you did not do so consensually, and therefore you were not to blame. The person who copied your answers is the one to blame. Or imagine that you were walking on a street in New York City and someone came up and stole your purse. You were the victim, you did not consent; therefore you are not to blame.

You must think of your involvement in date rape in the same way. You were there, and you were involved, but you did not give your consent. You were the victim. Some people will say that you deserved what happened because you had been drinking or you went to his apartment. But they do not say similar things to the person whose paper was copied or the person who was robbed. They do not say, "Well, if you hadn't been sitting in that seat it wouldn't have happened; therefore you deserve it"; nor, "You know New York City is dangerous, you shouldn't have gone there in the first place, but since you did you deserved to have your purse stolen." But they do make such statements to a victim of date or acquaintance rape, blaming her for her manner of dress, the amount she had drunk, the place, and her previous sexual experience. Sometimes people say, "What's the big deal? You had sex with him before often enough." Wouldn't such a statement be ridiculous if it were applied to the robbery victim? "Why are you complaining about being robbed; don't you give money to charities all the time?" In one situation the person is acting voluntarily; in the other the person is being forced. When you are forced, you are not to blame for what occurs; if you are acting voluntarily you are accountable for what happens.

The best way to put such an experience in perspective is to understand your feelings and the feelings of those around you. You need to be prepared for the emotional turmoil that will accompany your telling others about the event. Even though the rape happened to you, your whole family may feel very upset and act as if they have been victims.

Other people may treat you as if you are bad, or as if you deserved what happened because of some previous behavior on your part (like going to his apartment). It is important that you know that you were not to blame, that you were a victim, and that you are not bad or loose because you were raped. It is also important that you try to figure out in advance who will be able and willing to help you and who will blame you. Perhaps most important, you should know what your rights are and where you can go to get help. These matters are discussed in Chapter VII.

How Are You Feeling...

You are probably experiencing a variety of emotions about yourself and the people around you. You may not believe that it happened, or you may be numb, or angry, or embarrassed, or ashamed. You may not able to understand or explain many of these feelings, but they are there and important for you to deal with.

...About the Person Who Raped You?

How are you feeling about the person who raped you? Remember, he did it to you; you did not do it to yourself, and you did not do it to him. You are probably angry, but you may think your anger is unjustified because you were partly to blame. He raped you, and so he *does* deserve any anger you are feeling. You may think that because he is a nice man, or because you have known him for a long time he couldn't have done such a terrible thing to you. After all, nice men don't rape, and so what happened must not have been rape because he is a friend of the family, or your brother's best friend. You may think that someone you cared for so intensely would not do such a thing to you. It's hard to face the fact that he did not care for you as you did for him.

The fact that you knew him and felt positive about him may keep you from believing that what happened was rape, or that he could have done anything to hurt you on purpose. Therefore, you may feel that if he didn't behave inappropriately, it must have been you that did. You may tell yourself that your behavior gave him permission to force you to have sex, and so he was not wrong, you were. So you end up feeling that you deserved everything you got.

...About the World?

When you come to terms with the fact that someone you knew and trusted and perhaps even cared for a great deal raped you, you may be questioning your understanding of the world. You used to think you had good judgment, but maybe you didn't if you chose that man to spend time with; you trusted him, and look what happened. If you had had better judgment you wouldn't have chosen him as some-one desirable and safe to spend time with.

So now you may be questioning your judgment all the time. What if you go out and you see him or someone who reminds you of him? How can you know what classes to take in school? They might even discuss the topic of rape in class. He or his friends may be in those classes. Some date rape victims are worried about every decision they make, feeling that their judgment is so poor that they may make a similar or worse mistake in the future. Therefore they stop doing things that require decisions, which means that they pretty much stop doing anything. Trust in personal judgment and in others is gone. This is especially likely if the victim told her family or friends about the rape and they blamed her for it or did not believe her.

. . . About Your Family?

Your family is the one place you will probably hope to turn for support, but you may not feel that you can tell them. How will they react? Will they blame you? Some families respond better than the victim thought they would; some do not respond as well.

You must decide for yourself whether to tell your family. In general, it is best to tell at least one family member so that you have an ally to help you make decisions and support you during difficult periods. Family members may be able to think things through and give advice when decisions are hard for you to make, but the decisions must be yours. Do not do what someone else advises unless it feels like the right thing to do. If you respond in a way that is against your best judgment, you are likely to blame the one who advised you if the outcome is negative.

Regardless of the outcome of your decisions after rape, they must be yours. That does not mean that you shouldn't seek advice and information before making a decision. But it would be unwise to seek advice from someone who would be disappointed if you chose another route. Your adviser must be someone who can and will support you regardless of the decisions you make.

Some families react in a nonsupportive way because they

do not know how to be helpful. They may be embarrassed, frightened for you, angry at the situation, angry at you for putting them through it, or they may feel helpless. If this is is the way they respond, you must find someone who can give you emotional support. The local Rape Crisis Center will have counselors who can help you deal with this crisis. Your parents, friends, or significant other (boyfriend or girlfriend) may also be able to find help there in dealing with the fact that you are a rape victim. With this support they may become more understanding of your situation and more supportive of you.

. . . About Your Friends?

Your friends may be good resources for you, and they may be able to help you make good decisions. They are likely to have your best interests at heart without expecting anything from you. It is important for you to know how your friends think about date rape before you turn to them for help.

Some women friends may not be able to be as helpful as you would like. If your friends are like you in many ways, they may sense that if you were the victim of date rape, they also might be vulnerable. For that reason they may not want to believe that you were really raped, or they may believe that you were raped but that it was your fault. A friend with whom you are almost identical in interests, tastes, and behavior may want to believe that the only reason you were raped is because you did something to deserve it. Such a friend will not have to feel so vulnerable because she will think that she can avoid rape by avoiding that behavior.

Another reason such a friend may not be very helpful is that she may have been raped in the past. She may have been trying to forget the rape, and now you are reminding her of it. Therefore, she may not want or be able to help you.

Friends may not be helpful in ways you want. They may want you to press charges and have the rapist punished. If you don't want to go to the police, you may feel forced and coerced again by a "friend." Friends can be most supportive by letting you know that they still feel positively about you and want to help in whatever way you need. The help must be what *you* want, not what they want, because your regaining control over your life is the only way for you to recover.

Some men may feel bad that they were not able to protect you from the rape. Some may think that you invited the rape by your actions and therefore they may blame you. You do not have to have people around you who blame you or make you feel guilty. If you are uncomfortable with any of the people who want to help you, you have a right to insist that they leave. A representative from the Rape Crisis Center may be able to help you assert your rights if you are having trouble doing it by yourself.

You may feel angry at your friends for not believing you and not supporting you. You may think that they should know what you wanted and how you would respond in a dating situation, since you have discussed it with them so often. They may be making you feel worse than you already feel. YOU DO NOT HAVE TO LISTEN TO THEM, BELIEVE THEM, OR SPEND TIME WITH THEM! You need to make decisions that are the best for you. The first thing you need to do is heal, and then if you have the energy and interest you can decide how to deal with your anger at your friends.

CHAPTER 5

Whose Fault Is It?

Many people who are involved in acquaintance rape are unsure where the fault lies. Victims often assume the blame for having done something that they believe contributed to the rape, such as being drunk, or going to an isolated place with the rapist. Many assailants don't believe that what they did was rape. They think it was just a sexual situation in which the victim needed a little "push." The assailant often believes that the victim really wanted sex but couldn't acknowledge her desire because she was worried about her reputation. Therefore, if he pushes her to have sex, even if she says no, he assumes that he is doing her a favor by giving her what she wants. Some men just don't believe that a a woman ever means no.

The Person Who Rapes Is Responsible

In reality, the person who commits the crime is responsible for it. If the man forced, threatened, used violence, or coerced the woman to have sex, it was *rape*. It does not matter if the woman has no bruises, or if she had had sex with him before. Anytime a person is forced to have sex it is a crime.

Susan Estrich in her book *Real Rape* describes a hypothetical situation in which a person takes your car that is parked in front of your home. The car was unlocked. Was that the crime of grand larceny? Yes. Would it be grand larceny if you knew the person who took your car? Yes. Would it be grand larceny if you had allowed the person to drive it six months ago? Yes. You do not have to fight the person off and come away with bruises to call this a crime. You do not have to clearly tell everyone who admires your car that they may not take it. Your lack of consent is implied. The person who took your car took something from you without your consent.

We should apply the same standards to a rape situation. If an assailant "takes" sex from you without your consent and against your will, the situation is rape. It doesn't matter how well you know the person. You were not asking to have your car stolen because you left it unlocked. Similarly, women are not asking to be raped when they have been drinking.

Legal Responses

Although acquaintance rape and date rape are against the law, law enforcement officials often fail to treat incidents of rape for what they are. Police are most likely to believe that you are a victim of rape if you are a young woman, have bruises or injuries, don't know the assailant, didn't do anything (in their biased view) to "contribute" to the rape; report the crime to the police immediately; are hysterical immediately following the rape; and have medical evidence collected within a few hours of the rape.

Because of the nature of the crime, many victims do not

report to the police at all. If they ever do report the rape it may be months or years later. Of course, if you don't think that what has happened to you was rape, you will neither report to the police immediately nor have medical evidence collected. Many women don't identify what has happened to them as rape until an authority on the subject identifies it as rape and against the law.

Even though a woman may not describe what happened to her as rape, she may still feel like a victim. She may be experiencing the rape trauma syndrome. In the first phase of this syndrome the victim may react hysterically (crying uncontrollably, screaming, not wanting to be touched) or she may be stunned. The stunned reaction may be mistaken by the nonmedical observer as calm. This may lead police and inexperienced medical personnel to believe that she is fine emotionally. Thus they may believe that she couldn't be a rape victim, when in fact her response is typical.

Many police officers have difficulty believing a woman who says she has been raped if they believe the rape myths (see Chapter I) and do not understand the patterns of behavior that lead to acquaintance rape. Therefore, many victims of acquaintance rape face being told that their case is unfounded or that there is not enough evidence to present to the district attorney.

Police are also not likely to believe men who have been victims of sexual assault. If a man has been a victim of assault by an acquaintance (forced intercourse, oral sex, or anal sex), he is very unlikely to report it to the police. Some men feel that their masculinity is in question if they were overpowered by another man. Some men worry that they may be gay and that that somehow explains why another man would sexually assault them. They need to understand that men who force other men to have sex do so not primarily for sexual pleasure, but to dominate someone.

If a man is sexually victimized it doesn't, in fact, mean anything about his masculinity. It means that he was sought out as an object of domination. But if a man is worried that he may be a "latent homosexual,"* and his fears are verified by the fact that he was assaulted by another man, he may not want to report the crime for fear that others will believe he is homosexual. If he believes that rape is something that happens only to women, he begins to question his masculinity.

Social Responses

Most people in the United States believe the rape myths and thus are not likely to believe a victim of acquaintance rape.

Most women learn very early that it is not acceptable for them to fight or to hurt someone, especially if it is someone they care about and trust. Women also learn that it would be fruitless to try to defend themselves against someone bigger and stronger than they. Many date rapes are committed by someone the victim knows and trusts. She may believe that he will come to his senses at any moment and stop forcing her to have sex. It is a cruel but common distortion to hold a person responsible for an assault committed against him or her. Failing to fight back can't cause an assault.

Traditional societal patterns of sexual interaction assign to men the responsibility of initiating all dating and sexual encounters. A woman is expected to control sexual activity,

---

*The psychological community no longer believes in the concept of latent homosexuality. A person's sexual orientation is established in early childhood. One cannot be "turned" homosexual by engaging in one act of same-sex behavior. However, some less informed individuals may still believe that latent (potential) homosexuality is possible.

although she is rarely given any specific training in how to do it. A woman must keep her wits about her at all times if she is to control a sexual situation. But she is also expected to cooperate socially and make sure her date is having fun. If a woman drinks what he offers her, she may lose her ability to defend herself against his advances. Although she is not forcing him to have intercourse, people often say it is her fault for not stopping it, rather than his fault for pushing her beyond a point where she is comfortable. People are likely to say that a man was so drunk he couldn't control himself, but women are expected to control themselves and their dates whether they are drunk or not.

Although many people think that a man who is drunk can't control himself sexually, the law does not recognize drunkenness as permission to rape. Thoughtful people put the blame on the man, whose actions constitute rape, rather than on the woman who is unable to stop him.

Another behavior for which a woman is unfairly blamed is going to a man's apartment or inviting him to hers, especially on the first date. Inviting him for coffee usually means that she is offering him coffee, nothing more. He, however, may interpret it as an invitation to sex. Many who believe the rape myths blame her for being alone with him. After all, they say, she is supposed to control the situation and keep it from getting out of hand sexually. If she ends up in an isolated place and is forced to have sex, it is her fault for not remaining in a safer environment.

The woman may even be blamed for being a tease and leading him on. Some insist that there is only one reason for a man and a woman to be alone in an apartment, and that is for sex. So if she allows them to be alone, especially on a first date, she is leading him on and deserves whatever she gets. People who believe these ideas blame the victim for something she usually cannot control. What if a woman has sex with many men? Traditionally female virginity is considered desirable before marriage. If you are not a virgin before marriage, you are "spoiled goods." Why does it make a difference if you have sex with more than one person? On the other hand, many believe the woman is even more at fault if she has had many partners. For example, some believe that a prostitute cannot be raped; presumably because she has had sex with many men she has given up her right to say no. In fact, prostitutes can be raped. Any woman can be raped, no matter how many men she has had as sexual partners. The number of sexual partners is irrelevant, and the relationship she has with the man is also irrelevant. She may even be raped by a man with whom she has had consensual sex in the past. Anytime a woman does not want to have sex but is forced to do so, that act is rape.

Another common myth is that a woman is responsible for a man's sexual excitement, especially if she did something to turn him on. The fact is that we are all responsible for our own sexual excitement. The limbic system of the brain, which controls emotion, turns us on and off sexually. A partner may be the stimulus, but it is our own brain that turns us on and off. Therefore if a woman kisses her partner, even if he becomes sexually excited, he has no right to conclude that she intends to have intercourse with him. However, she may mistakenly feel responsible for helping him relieve his sexual tension and think she should have intercourse with him if he becomes sexually excited in response to her stimulation. She is under no obligation to do this.

What if a woman says no but the man doesn't believe she means it. Should she have to say it more than once? Some men don't admit that a woman ever means no. Others need to have the no accompanied by a convincing and specific action to believe it. In other words, if you say no but giggle or let him continue to unbutton your blouse, he is less likely to pay attention to your no. Does this give him the right to force sex? No! However, he may think that you really want sex because your body language is different from your verbal message. He also may not hear your no if he has been drinking or if he feels that he has a right to sex because you "led him on."

Some young women have a reputation for being sexually promiscuous, whether deserved or not. If a man believes that you have had sex with every other man on the basketball team but you won't sleep with him, he may feel angry and rejected. If he forces you to have sex under those circumstances, it is rape. He may feel justified, however, and others may condone his behavior even though no one has the right to force sex on anyone.

Safety Decreases with Increased Vulnerability

Some things that women do can increase their vulnerability to sexual assault. Although it is never a woman's fault if she is raped, there are ways in which she can increase her safety. Whether or not you have used any prevention strategy, you are *not* to blame if rape occurs. But because it is desirable to decrease your vulnerability, you may want to think about the suggestions that follow.

How Were You Vulnerable?

If you were raped you may have done something that your friends or your own brain tell you was stupid, something that in retrospect you wish you hadn't done. If this is so, you should identify the behavior and avoid it under similar circumstances in the future. Does this mean that you cannot ever kiss a man again, or have a drink? No. What it means is that because some of your actions may decrease your reasoning ability, or be incorrectly interpreted by others, you need to increase your safety in these situations.

For instance, if you are at a party with a girlfriend who drove and you don't know any other people there, make sure you know where your friend is, and when she is leaving. Don't be left behind and have to count on someone you just met to take you home. He could rape you in the car.

Remember several important points about your behavior at a party: (1) don't get so drunk that you can't keep track of your friend's whereabouts (she may be drinking too); (2) don't go to a secluded place with someone you have just met; (3) always have cab or bus fare in the event that your ride does leave without you, and know how late public transportation is available; and (4) don't rely on someone you have just met to give you a ride.

Suppose you are at a party and you want to be alone with someone, perhaps because there is too much noise to talk. Be sure to tell the friend you came with that you are going to another room, how long you expect to be there, and the name of the person you will be with. For example, you may say, "Jane, I am going upstairs with Jim Ellis to see his room. We will be there for about fifteen minutes. Please come and get me if you are ready to go before I come down." That way Jim knows that you only plan to spend a short time alone with him, and your friend knows where to find you. This is a good strategy if you feel you must go to his room, but it would be much better not to go to a secluded place with someone you don't know well.

It is important to remember that acquaintance rape or date rape sometimes happens when people have just met each other, but sometimes the assailant has known the victim for years. He may be your teacher, or your boss, or your friend. If you are with someone who begins to become "too familiar" (does suggestive or sexual things that make you uncomfortable), it may be a sign that he will go too far if he has the opportunity. Thus the same principles apply to people you have known for some time, even someone you may have been dating, as well as to people you have just met.

What if you are kissing your date and really enjoying it, and then he starts to "fool around." You may enjoy that too but not be sure you should be doing it; so you make a feeble attempt to say no, but you don't sound as if you mean it because you are not sure you want to stop. He doesn't stop. He goes on to try to unbutton your pants. You have been telling him no without meaning it for the last half hour, but now you really want him to stop. This time you say no more forcefully, but he still thinks you mean yes, so he continues against your wishes. By telling him no without meaning it you encourage him to believe that your no means yes. It is important to say what you mean. If you are not sure, tell him that you don't know what you want but that he should believe that no means no when you say it.

Let's say you want to take a man to your apartment to "fool around" with him, but you don't want to have intercourse. What can you do? First you should tell him what your limits are. Don't take him to an empty apartment. Be sure your roommates are there. If you have asked them to come if you call for help, they may be able to help you to control the situation.

These are some examples of how a woman's behavior may contribute to her vulnerability. Many more suggestions are offered in Chapter VIII. But remember, no matter what behaviors you engage in, you are never responsible for a crime that someone else commits against you.

It is important to understand where the blame and responsibility lie for acquaintance rape and sexual assault. Because the person you are with misinterprets your behavior and believes that you want sex does not give him the right to force you to have sex. No one has the right to force you to have sex.

You may encounter people who say that you can cause rape by your behavior. They are wrong. They may also diminish the importance of rape because they believe that sex is just sex and no big deal if you have had sex before. They do not understand the causes of rape, or the devastating effects it can have on the victim.

Some friends may tell you that forced sex with a date is not as serious as stranger rape when a maniac jumps out of the bushes and rapes you brutally. This is wrong! Both stranger rape and acquaintance rape are emotionally difficult for the victim. Stranger rape may be more traumatic physically, but acquaintance rape is often more traumatic emotionally, partly because a woman may no longer feel able to trust her own judgment. She may not be able to trust men anymore. She may not have the support and understanding of friends and family that would be likely in cases of stranger rape. The police are even less likely to believe her.

CHAPTER 6

Whom Should You Tell and Where Can You Go for Help?

I f you have been raped by an acquaintance you are probably wondering what you should do. Decision-making may be harder now than usual. Who will believe you? Who will say it was your fault? What if you are pregnant? How will you know if you have contracted a sexually transmissible disease? What should you do if you want to press charges and have him arrested? Where can you go for emotional help?

These are all important questions. Unfortunately, few people know much about acquaintance rape, and even fewer will be able to give you good advice. If you find people who know about acquaintance rape, how will you know if they can help you?

You may think that your friends and family are the best people to tell because they care about you and will help you to make good decisions. That may be true, but they will also have their own emotions about your having been raped, which may prevent them from giving you the kind of help you need.

Friends

The friends you may want to tell could be female or male. You may be thinking about telling your boyfriend or your best girlfriend or your roommates. These people may be supportive, but they also may have trouble dealing with your discomfort and pain and the reality of the fact that you were raped.

KIM

Kim was very religious and wanted to be a virgin when she got married. She and Scott had been going together for three years, since their junior year in high school. They went away to different colleges and saw each other on weekends about once a month. In between they did not date other people, though they both made new friends.

Kim was working on a small group project with John, a man in her sociology class, which required them to meet several times out of class. The fourth time they met was in Kim's dorm room. Her roommate was there too, but was having trouble concentrating on her studying with Kim and John talking, so she went to the library.

Once they were alone, John began to make sexual advances, which Kim resisted. She explained that she and Scott were dating and planned to marry after they graduated from college. John told her that she should experience other guys before she settled down with her high school sweetheart. She said that that was her decision and she did not want to date other guys. John said he knew she wanted it (meaning sex) because of the signals she was giving him when they were together working on the project. John forced Kim to have intercourse, ignoring her vehement protests.

John left immediately after he had finished, and Kim lay crying on her bed. She did not know what to do, so she called Scott, thinking that he would be able to comfort her and tell her what to do. To her surprise, Scott became very quiet and told her he needed time to think about things. He was hurt, disappointed, and confused. He decided to consult the priest on campus, but he was even more confused after talking to him.

It was important to Scott that he marry a virgin. Kim was no longer a virgin. And even though the priest said that the rape was not Kim's fault, Scott could not help but question why she had invited John to her room to study. He also believed that a woman should fight back to prevent a rape, and Kim didn't.

Although he still loved Kim, he could not bring himself to trust her or believe her. She was no longer the one he wanted to marry. Their relationship ended a few months later when Scott told Kim that he could only marry a virgin.

Even though Scott and Kim had a good relationship before the rape, Scott was not able to be helpful to Kim afterward. He had his own emotional problems to deal with. He knew very little about rape, and he blamed Kim for not being able to avoid it. His response was not only not helpful to Kim, it was harmful, because he added to her emotional burden. Although she was not to blame, she felt that she should have been able to avoid the rape and so blamed herself for not being stronger.

Kim needed the support of someone who knew enough about acquaintance rape to help her stop blaming herself and get the emotional and medical help that she needed. She also needed someone to help her decide whom to tell and how to tell them. In addition, she needed advice about her legal rights and what she should do regarding John. She did not want to see him again, but they were in the same sociology class. Scott was not able to give her any of this help, and he needed emotional help himself.

Feelings of guilt prevent many victims from telling others about the rape. Few acquaintance rape victims tell their parents immediately (although some do years later), but many tell their friends or siblings that they have had a "bad" sexual experience. It appears that the response of the first person who is told determines how the victim feels about the event in the future.

JANE

Jane was manager of the football team and really enjoyed the close friendships she had developed with many of the players, but she hadn't dated any of them.

One night Jane was asleep in bed when one of the players came to the apartment to see her. Her roommates told him that she was sleeping, but he convinced them that he was a good friend and she would be happy to see him. So they let him into her room.

Once in the room he climbed on the bed with Jane and started kissing her. She was startled when awakened and did not know what was happening.

Once she realized who he was, he was pulling the covers off. Jane could smell alcohol on his breath and thought he was drunk. She asked what he wanted, and he said, "You know." Jane didn't want to have sex with him, but she was afraid to tell him to stop because she thought he would hurt her.

Since he was drunk, it took him a long time to ejaculate, and he was hurting Jane with his clumsy attempts at intercourse. Jane was crying through the entire rape. When he finally came, he passed out on top of her and didn't wake up for several hours. Once he came to, he got dressed and left.

Jane staggered into her roommates' room and asked them how he had gotten in. When they said they had let him in, Jane was furious and said, "You let him in to rape me!" Their response was that it couldn't have been rape. She had been interested in having a relationship with him ever since she met him, so what was she complaining about?

Jane was devastated. She had been raped, and her best friends said that she was to blame.

Not all friends respond in negative ways when they are told about an acquaintance rape. But a person must be mature and know quite a bit about acquaintance rape to be helpful. Frequently it is better to seek help from older people who are informed about the topic. Parents, teachers, counselors, clergy, rape crisis counselors, doctors, or nurses may be helpful, but not all adults in those categories will be able to help. They may also have trouble dealing with their emotional response to the rape, or they may not know enough about acquaintance rape to be a good support person.

Family

Parents often say that they feel as if the whole family had been violated when one of their children is raped. This makes the victim feel that her very personal problems are being ignored. Some parents are able to put their feelings aside long enough to be helpful; others try to deny their feelings; and still others are too upset to be helpful at all.

ANNETTE

When Annette was a junior in high school, she accepted a ride home from school from a man who raped her. She had met the man through a mutual friend and was surprised to see him waiting for her after school one day. He offered her a ride, and she gladly accepted, especially because all her friends had seen him meet her in his sports car. He told her he wanted to take her home by the "scenic route." Several miles from her house he stopped the car in he woods, where he forced her to have intercourse. Then he drove her home.

When she got in the house, her mother started scolding because she was late. She told her mother what had happened, but her mother screamed that she was a sinner and needed to be saved. Her mother said that she deserved what she got for accepting a ride with a man none of them knew, and she should be ashamed for bringing disgrace upon the family.

Annette's mother was too distraught by her own feelings to be able to help Annette. She caused more problems for Annette by blaming her for the rape.

Before you tell a family member, you need to assess how

that person will be likely to react to your rape. It should be someone who has usually been able to help in other situations, who is concerned about you, and who wants you to get over whatever problems you have. It is important to remember that you are the most important person right now. Don't confide in people or ask them for help just because you think their feelings would be hurt if you didn't ask.

TIFFANY

Tiffany was raped by a date when she was in high school. She was very upset and wanted to tell someone, but she was worried about how her family would deal with the aftermath of rape. She was afraid that her brother would do something stupid, like beating up or even killing the man. She thought her mother would be a good support person, but she didn't want the entire family to know.

When she told her mother about the rape and her fears about her brother, her mother was very supportive. She helped Tiffany figure out how to get help without letting her brother know right away. Several years later when Tiffany had healed fairly well from the emotional trauma of the rape, she told her brother about it. He was older and less hotheaded and was able to deal with his anger and frustration in a constructive way by being supportive to Tiffany. Her assailant had moved out of the community by then, so Tiffany didn't have to worry about her brother's doing something stupid for which he would be put in jail.

Tiffany's mother was helpful, but her brother would not have been if she had told him immediately after the rape.

She made a wise choice to keep it from him at that time, since he would have added to her worries rather than diminishing them.

Some family members may have very good intentions but turn out not to be the best people to help you. One mother whose daughter confided in her immediately after the rape went to the college and took over the decision-making because the daughter did not feel able to make decisions for herself. The attorneys representing the college suggested that the mother retain her own attorney to represent her daughter and suggested a local attorney. The mother was grateful for the advice and did hire that attorney. Unfortunately, he knew nothing about acquaintance rape and seemed to have the college's welfare in mind rather than the victim's. As a result the case was handled quietly and the victim's wishes were ignored. She wanted the assailant removed from campus so she would not have to see him during her normal daily routine. On the contrary the assailant was allowed to remain on campus, the victim dropped out of school, and the college received minimal negative publicity.

If the mother had not been so emotionally involved herself, she might have realized that it was not wise to hire an attorney recommended by the college. It is difficult for people who are emotionally involved with a victim of rape to think clearly. In a case like this, a professional such as a rape crisis counselor and a trusted family member or friend may be a good combination.

Rape Crisis Centers

Rape crisis counselors know from experience which attorneys, medical personnel, and therapists are qualified and able to be most helpful in specific cases. They are also able to work with all members of the family or friends who are involved.

If you call a Rape Crisis Center you will talk with a highly trained counselor over the phone. You do not have to identify yourself, so you can talk for a while to see if you feel comfortable with him or her. If so, you may ask the counselor to meet you at your home, the hospital, or any other place to decide what to do next. The counselor will not tell you what to do but will advise you of your options. The decision-making is up to you, and the counselor will support you in whatever you decide.

Rape crisis counselors are generally the most specialized counselors available to you, and rape crisis services are free. These counselors will work with you as long as you need it, advising you on legal issues, going to the hospital or to court with you, and helping you to return to a normal life. Although counselors in Rape Crisis Centers are well trained and empathetic, an individual counselor may not be the right one for you. If you are not having a positive experience with any counselor, you should change counselors.

Other Counselors

Therapists, medical personnel, and religious counselors may all be able to help after a rape, but not all are trained specifically in rape counseling. Even fewer are educated about acquaintance rape issues.

Therapists. The therapist who may be helpful to you may come from almost any group of professionally trained and recognized therapists. Many victims prefer to talk to a female therapist, but just because a therapist is female does not make her the right person for you. Some male therapists may be helpful in dealing with the aftermath of rape. If you are already seeing a therapist about other matters and have a good relationship with that person, you may want to discuss the rape with him or her. On the other hand, if he or she is not familiar with acquaintance rape issues or makes you feel uncomfortable, you may want to seek out someone who is. If your therapist does not know much about acquaintance rape, you may suggest that he or she contact the Rape Crisis Center. You may also want to recommend the book *The Rape Victim: Clinical and Community Approaches to Treatment* by Koss and Harvey.

You can find a therapist who knows about acquaintance rape by calling your local Rape Crisis Center and asking for a list of recommended therapists. It would be best to get several names, so that if you don't hit it off with the first person you have other options. Therapists listed in the Yellow Pages under sex therapy are not necessarily familiar with this issue. Select your therapist carefully, and do not continue with one who blames you for the rape or makes you feel guilty.

Medical Personnel. There are several sources of the immediate medical help you will need after rape, but the best is probably the emergency room of a hospital that has a special rape trauma team. This group of medical professionals may have a different title in your hospital, but such a team will be able to meet your needs much better than those untrained in sexual assault. The team will probably consist of a doctor, a nurse, a social worker, and perhaps a police officer. They will treat all your medical and emotional problems. They will be aware of your needs and be able to discover and treat injuries, even those that are difficult to observe such as inside the vagina. They will also collect specimens in such a way that they will be admissible in court if you decide to have the assailant charged with rape.

If there is a chance that you will accuse your assailant

legally, you need physical evidence collected by medically qualified personnel as soon after the rape as possible, at least within twelve hours. You should not do anything that could destroy evidence, such as washing your face or any part of your body, combing your hair, changing your clothes, brushing your teeth, gargling, or douching. Although wanting to cleanse your body to remove all evidence of the rape is a common emotional need, those actions will destroy evidence.

If you decide to proceed legally, even if you were not examined and do not have medical evidence, your opportunity is not necessarily lost. In many cases of acquaintance rape, the assailant admits that sexual intercourse occurred. The case will rest on whether the sexual intercourse was forced or nonconsensual.

Medical professionals who may be helpful to you include doctors, nurses, nurse practitioners, physician assistants, and medical social workers. You can receive adequate help from any of these people only if you feel comfortable with them, if they understand acquaintance rape issues, and if they are medically experienced in evidence collection and treatment of victims. These people can help with your physical needs, and they should also consider your emotional needs.

You may need extended emotional counseling that will cost significant amounts of money, as will the help you receive from trained therapists. Such long-term counseling will help you regain normal relationships in your personal life and is different from the crisis counseling you receive immediately after the rape.

Religious Counselors. These professionals are more likely to help you free of charge if counseling is part of their ministry. The same criteria apply as with the other professionals regarding their potential helpfulness. You should feel comfortable with them, they should understand acquaintance rape issues, and they should have training in counseling. These people may be clerical or lay counselors of your religion.

Regardless of whom you choose to confide in, it is important that they be truly helpful to you. You should feel free to change counselors or stop going to anyone who you feel is not being helpful. You must do whatever you need to do to help yourself regain a normal life.

The Police

You may choose to utilize the legal system after an acquaintance rape. Most victims do not for a variety of reasons. Perhaps they do not want their private life exposed to the world with little chance of obtaining a conviction. Perhaps they feel guilty about what they see as their contribution to the rape. Perhaps they do not want to be responsible for ruining the assailant's life. Perhaps it was weeks or months before they were willing to admit they were raped.

Reporting rape to law enforcement officials is the focus of the next chapter; however, use of officers or investigators as counselors is discussed here. Some law enforcement officials are specifically trained in stranger and acquaintance rape issues. These officers, who are usually female but not always, may be helpful in informing you of your legal rights. They may tell you that because of the low conviction rate obtained by the district attorney in your community, there is a slim chance of obtaining a conviction if you decide to press charges. They may be able to direct you to medical professionals or therapists. They may just be available to listen to you and give you suggestions for making your environment safer. You may want to develop a friendly relationship with the officer so that you will have someone to call if you want reassurance or if you are in danger in the future.

In any event the final decision is yours whether to press charges. If you do, the police officer will take your statement, collect evidence, and turn the information over to the district attorney. The quality and quantity of the evidence will help the district attorney decide if the case should be sent to the grand jury, so you should provide as much evidence as possible. In addition to the information the police officer obtains from you, physical and medical evidence will make your case stronger. Seeking medical help immediately after a rape may be helpful for that reason and also be important for your long-term physical well-being.

Medical Care

You should seek medical care after being raped by a stranger or an acquaintance because you may have been injured internally. There may be tears of the vaginal or rectal tissue, depending on the activity you were forced to perform. In addition, you may become pregnant or you may have contracted a sexually transmitted disease. Therefore, even if you decide not to press charges, you should receive medical care for your own health. If you decide later that you want to press charges, the evidence will be available, and the police and the prosecutor are more likely to believe you if medical evidence was collected.

Physical Trauma and Pregnancy Prevention

If you do go for medical care, you can be treated within seventy-two hours to prevent pregnancy and at any time for sexually transmissible diseases. The sooner the better, however, especially if there are internal injuries that require treatment. Pregnancy is not a common outcome of rape, but it occasionally occurs. You may wish to ask for the "morning after" pill to prevent pregnancy, but you should find out about possible side effects such as nausea before you accept a prescription. This medication is available only from clinicians and contains high levels of female hormones. Decisions about pregnancy may also be made if and when pregnancy is confirmed.

Sexually Transmissible Disease Prevention

Treatment for sexually transmissible diseases (STDs) usually includes an antibiotic at the time of the first visit, with several follow-up visits to make sure that a disease has not developed weeks or months after the rape. The follow-up visits are important because some STDs have long incubation periods and may not be detectable within the first few weeks after the rape. Since anyone can have a sexually transmissible disease, you are not immune even if the person who raped you was rich, handsome, or intelligent. As a matter of fact, since those who commit acquaintance rape are often promiscuous, he is probably at high risk for having an STD.

CHAPTER 7

What Are Your Rights?

A cquaintance rape and date rape are against the law. All rape is against the law, but the law has not been applied consistently. There are two ways you can get redress under the law as an acquaintance rape victim. You may seek criminal prosecution or file a civil suit. Information on the difference between the two is given later in the chapter.

Victims, assailants, the general public, and the law tend to consider acquaintance rape less significant than stranger rape. The degree of violence and force used, a prior relationship with the assailant, and the degree of post-rape hysteria are common and erroneous criteria used to determine whether rape occurred and how it should be treated legally. The victim's past sexual history and her socio-economic status are other factors in erroneous judgments about a rape victim's credibility.

What Is the Law

Legal statutes regarding rape vary from state to state. In some states rape is defined as forced intercourse committed by a man on a woman. Other states have much broader definitions: either sex can be either the victim or the assailant, and forced sex acts other than sexual intercourse are covered. Some states do not mention the crime of rape in their statutes but may use more general terms such as sexual assault or sexual abuse. In about half of the states a woman cannot legally charge her husband with rape. The laws that exclude marital rape were written in the past when a woman was considered the property of her husband, and he could have sex with his wife anytime he wanted. In many states the term rape may not be used if the victim is male; under the law a rape victim may only be female. In those states, sex forced on a man is considered sexual assault.

In many states an act is considered rape or sexual assault if it is against the woman's will and without her consent. A woman has not consented if she says no or if she is drunk or unconscious, asleep, too young to know what she is consenting to, or mentally incompetent. A man who decides that a woman is "asking for it" by being drunk so he has a right to sex if she has passed out may find himself charged with rape.

Because state laws differ so greatly, you must check the laws of your state to see what is considered rape or sexual assault. You can find out by contacting a local police agency, a chapter of the National Organization for Women, a Rape Crisis Center, the district attorney's office, an attorney, or a pro-bono legal clinic (free legal services offered by most law schools and by lawyers in most cities).

If you have been sexually assaulted or raped, you should

know exactly where the violation falls within the law. You may have, in fact, been raped; but if you are married to the assailant the act may *not* be against the law where you live. Similarly, if you are a male victim of forced oral or anal sex, the attack may not be considered rape, but it may be considered sodomy or sexual assault. In some places the law states that a woman need only be in fear for her safety or her life for a sexual encounter to be considered rape.

Some people refer to "victim-precipitated" rape, meaning that the woman was partially to blame, or "asked for it." Legal distinctions are often drawn between "simple" rape and "aggravated" rape. Simple rape is one in which there is no evidence of violence, threats, or a struggle. This is often the case when the victim and assailant know each other. Aggravated rape is one in which a weapon, threat, violence, or force is used or there is more than one assailant. Members of the legal community are less likely to accept simple rape for prosecution than aggravated rape. This does not mean that simple rape is not a crime, but fewer people view simple rape as a crime, and it is more difficult to prove in court.

DIANA

Diana had known Brad for several months, and they were part of a peer group. After having attended a play with their friends, Brad asked Diana to have a late supper with him. He was really "turned on" by her sexy dress and wanted to get to know her better. She was also interested in getting to know Brad, since she had been attracted to him for months.

They went to a quiet little Italian restaurant, where they shared two bottles of wine and talked for hours. Diana invited Brad to her house for a nightcap. After several drinks, Brad suggested that he give her a hot oil back rub. It sounded wonderful to her, so she agreed to undress and wrap herself in a towel. Brad told her she had nothing to worry about, because he was a minister's son and had only honorable intentions.

Halfway through the back rub Brad started kissing her neck, which felt delightful. They enjoyed kissing and fooling around for almost an hour. Suddenly Brad became forceful and told Diana to remove the towel completely. She resisted seriously until Brad grabbed her arms very roughly and raised his voice.

Diana was very frightened. She knew no one would hear her if she screamed because she was alone for the weekend in a secluded house. Brad forced her to have oral sex and intercourse. Diana did not resist; she remained still, almost as if dead, throughout. She felt as if she were across the room watching the rape. She couldn't believe it was happening to her.

After Brad left she locked the door, took a long, hot shower, and went to bed. She couldn't sleep the entire night. The next day her roommates came home and found her acting like a zombie. They knew something was wrong, but Diana wouldn't tell them what had happened until after hours of questioning. They then persuaded her to go to the police to report the rape.

At the police station she was questioned by a uniformed male officer who insisted that she describe all the details of her dress, how much she had had to drink, and what had happened. He seemed to enjoy the details of the sexual encounter. When he had finished taking the report he told Diana to take his advice and go home and forget all about it. "You really expect me to believe that you didn't want it after you

invited him to your place and you undressed willingly? What did you expect him to do, play cards? The
district attorney would laugh at me if I presented this
case to him. Do yourself a favor, don't take any more
men home!"

This officer probably didn't believe that what happened
was really rape, but in any case he thought she deserved it
for "leading him on." No one who has been sexually assault
ed is responsible for it, but many people think that certain
behavior gives a rapist permission to rape. Although more
and more police, district attorneys, and judges understand
that there is no such thing as "victim precipitation," many
still believe there is.

What Can You Expect from the Legal System?

You will deal with a number of people and organizations if
you go to the police. First, you may contact the police or an
attorney to determine what the laws are in your state. You
may contact the police to report the crime (so that they
have a description of the attacker and his pattern of behavior), even if you don't want to press charges. If you do
want to press charges, you will have to talk with a uniformed officer and a detective or an investigator, so that
they can gather evidence pertinent to the case. In a criminal proceeding the district attorney will then become
involved to determine if there is enough evidence to seek
an indictment from the grand jury. If an indictment is
handed down, the case will go to court, and you will be
confronted with the prosecuting attorney, the defense
attorney, the jury, and the judge during the trial.

Most acquaintance rape cases are not reported to the

police. Of those that are reported, very few end up in court.

Will They Prosecute My Case?

The police may feel that there is not enough evidence to turn the case over to the district attorney, or they may feel that it was victim-precipitated rape, implying that you were as much to blame as the rapist. If the case does reach the district attorney, it may be dropped at that point as not being strong enough for an indictment.

Of the acquaintance rape cases that actually go to trial, few result in conviction. This is because juries are made up of people who believe many of the rape myths discussed in Chapter I. In addition, members of the jury may have been in similar situations in which sex was forced, but they did not consider it rape. Men are understandably reluctant to define someone else's behavior as rape if they have done the same thing and do not consider themselves rapists. Women on juries may be hard on an acquaintance rape victim, wanting to dissociate themselves from such vulnerability and finding it easier to blame the victim.

In some cases the jury is in agreement that sexual intercourse occurred but disagrees over the issue of consent. If the jury is not convinced beyond a reasonable doubt that the woman was forced, they are reluctant to convict the man for a "misunderstanding."

Many rape victims choose to interact with the legal system by informing themselves about the law and getting advice as to the wisdom of seeking prosecution. You may want to ask if there is a specially trained rape task force representative who will be understanding. You may also want to ask for a female officer.

Judith Rowland, a former Assistant District Attorney, has written the book *The Ultimate Violation*, in which she describes her experiences in attempting to obtain convictions in acquaintance rape cases. She succeeded in some cases by using expert witnesses to demonstrate the rape trauma syndrome. She had therapists and psychiatrists examine the victim and testify that she had experienced the rape trauma syndrome immediately after the rape, contrasted to her emotional condition before the rape, which was normal. The jury concluded that the forced sex she experienced was rape. The rape trauma syndrome is described in Chapter IV.

Criminal Cases

If you seek criminal prosecution and the district attorney takes your case, the law acts as if the rapist had violated the members of your community by breaking the community law. The case becomes the people of your State vs. the rapist. You become only a witness for the State. The district attorney may not take your case if he or she believes that it is weak or that no crime was committed.

If you are successful in a criminal case, the assailant is found guilty. He may receive a suspended sentence or probation, be required to perform community service, or be sent to prison.

Unfortunately, the likelihood of a guilty verdict in an acquaintance rape case is very small. If you seek criminal prosecution and then lose, you may feel more out of control and helpless than before the trial. You should be aware that your personal life and morality may be described in detail in the courtroom and verbally attacked by the rapist's attorney.

Most states have laws to protect the victim from having

her entire past sexual history revealed in court. These laws are called Rape Shield laws. Generally they allow only sexual information related to the case being tried to be revealed in court. An assailant's past criminal record may not be presented in court even if he has been convicted of a similar crime. These legal provisions are made to avoid prejudicing the jury.

The Rape Shield laws do help protect both the victim and the assailant. If the victim knew that her past sexual history would be revealed in court, it might keep her from going to court. Similarly, if the assailant's record were revealed in court and he had raped before, the jury might convict him based on his record, not on the merits of the case. So the laws are designed to provide a fair and impartial trial, and they usually work.

Civil Cases

Because it is so difficult to obtain a criminal conviction, some acquaintance rape victims turn to the civil courts. Criminal conviction requires unanimous decision by the jury that they have been convinced beyond a reasonable doubt that the defendant committed the crime. Often in a civil court only a majority of the jurors have to be convinced that the defendant is guilty, but that depends on where the case is heard. If the victim wins or settles out of court, she usually receives a financial award.

In a civil case the victim is suing the assailant personally. The state is not involved. The victim retains an attorney, who usually charges a percentage of the award the victim receives, usually about 30 percent. The major difference between a civil and a criminal case is the standard of proof required. In a civil case one need only prove a preponderance of probability, rather than beyond a reasonable doubt as in a criminal case. With the same evidence, it is usually easier to win a civil suit than a criminal suit.

Some victims choose to sue someone other than the assailant, charging failure to provide them with protection, especially if the assailant has no money. For example, suppose a woman broke up with her boyfriend, but he refused to return the key to her apartment. She asked the landlord to change the lock but he didn't, and the ex-boyfriend let himself in and raped her. Such a victim may sue the landlord, claiming that his negligence caused the attack.

If an eighteen-year-old college woman gets drunk at a school function and is raped while she is passed out, she may sue the institution for failing to provide a safe, alcohol-free environment or for failing to prevent alcohol consumption by minors.

What About Medical and Therapy Costs?

In many places you may be eligible for compensation for the costs of medical expenses if you press charges and the case goes to court. The district attorney's office will pay for the medical expenses related to evidence collection. Any costs you may have for emotional or psychological therapy do not fall into that category unless you need a psychiatric evaluation for medical evidence. Long-term therapy costs are not covered.

If you decide not to seek prosecution, you may be able to recover costs by applying to the crime victims' compensation board in your community. Unfortunately, not all communities have such boards. Since the medical costs can be high (initial hospital costs, follow-up medical tests, therapy, etc.), it makes good sense to apply for such help if it is available.

If you decide to seek criminal prosecution, you will not

have legal costs because the district attorney represents the state (and you).

It is important to remember that each case is different, and the situation and the evidence in your case may make it easy to win. If violence was involved you probably will have an easier time in court.

CHAPTER 8

Preventing Rape

T here are a number of things you can do to keep yourself from becoming a victim of acquaintance rape.
These strategies and suggestions apply to those who
have never been victims as well as those who have but
want to avoid rape again. They are also appropriate to help
men become less vulnerable to sexual assault.

This chapter focuses on potential victims. Suggestions
for how to avoid being an assailant are given in Chapter X.
You can prevent acquaintance rape on two levels. First,
you can make yourself safer. These suggestions apply to
almost everyone. Second, you can make the world safer for
others. Although these suggestions may be employed by
anyone, they are most appropriate for those who have been
raped, because of their unique insight into rape from the
victim's point of view.

THINGS YOU CAN DO FOR YOURSELF

Feel Good About Yourself

If you do not feel good about yourself, you probably don't
think you have a right to ask others to stop doing things

they want to do. For example, if you are with a partner who wants sexual intercourse and you only want to kiss, you may assume that your partner has a greater right to his wishes. If you felt good about yourself you would not feel that you had to stay with someone who wanted you to do things against your wishes.

Get Emotional Help

But feeling good about yourself may be easier said than done. If you do not feel good about yourself, you must first identify the reasons you are feeling bad before you can do anything to correct the situation. For example, if you feel bad about the fact that you have been raped, perhaps professional counseling may help you to feel better. But you may also be able to gain the same benefits from talking to a sympathetic friend who will support rather than blame you.

Stay Away from Those Who Treat You Badly

If you do not like the way others are treating you, one strategy is to tell them what it is about their behavior that makes you uncomfortable, how it makes you feel, and how you would like them to change it. This is called an "I message." For example, suppose a friend makes fun of the way you wear your hair. You could say, "When you make fun of my hair (offensive behavior) I feel hurt and embarrassed (feelings). I would like you to stop commenting on my hair or to help me change my hair style so that we both like it (change message)."

Another possibility is for you to change the thing you are being teased about. Still another possibility is to change friends and surround yourself with people who will be nicer to you. This is not always possible, but perhaps you can minimize the amount of time you spend with people who make you uncomfortable.

No matter what it is that is making you feel bad about yourself, there are people and groups in your community that can help you: school counselors, rape crisis counselors, crisis hotlines, departments of social services, drug or alcohol programs, weight control centers, physical fitness centers, and many others. You can find many of them in the Yellow Pages of the phone book, or by calling a crisis hotline, which will have referral phone numbers for many of the services you may need. Remember, the best way to feel better about yourself is to find out what is making you feel bad and try to change it.

You Have a Right to Be Respected

You have a right to be respected and to have your wishes respected. If you want to go to a specific place or to do something in particular on a date, you should be able to do those things unless they are in conflict with the wishes of the other person or are immoral or illegal. An immoral behavior would be doing something wrong such as not telling your date if you have a sexually transmissible disease (such as herpes) before sex. If the other person wants to do something different, the two of you should negotiate, compromise, or at least agree on the activity and location of the date. If your date is not willing to take your wishes seriously or to compromise, he has only his interests in mind. He is not interested in you or your welfare. If you are with someone who does not seem to be interested in your welfare, stop spending time with him!

Be Careful About Alcohol

Alcohol is frequently present in acquaintance rape situations. Alcohol dulls the senses and impairs your ability to assess situations. It may make you oblivious to the increasing danger of a situation. For example, you may not be aware that your ride has left the party and that you have no way to get home. Or you may mistakenly presume that you are strong enough physically to stop someone from forcing you to have sex. In addition, alcohol decreases inhibitions and may change your date's perceptions so that he thinks he should respond to your refusal in a macho manner and force you to do what he wants.

People often use drinking as an excuse for bad behavior. If you are with a man who is drunk, he may say that he couldn't help himself because the alcohol clouded his judgment and he got "carried away." People sometimes say that a woman who was raped deserved if because she was drunk. Thus, alcohol is sometimes used to excuse men and to blame women for rape, and by women to blame themselves for the situation.

Mean What You Say and Say What You Mean

Often, women and men do not really mean what they say. Women are brought up to be nice and try to please everyone. Men are taught to take charge. Therefore women are afraid to make an angry statement lest it hurt or annoy others, especially a man who feels he should be in charge. So women often try to say difficult things in a nice way, deny their feelings, or not say anything at all.

For example, if a woman feels that a man is getting too intimate on the dance floor, she will probably not tell him how she feels. If he asks her if something is wrong, she may say, "No, it's getting hot in here; let's go outside and cool off." She is denying her feelings and trying to reject his advances in a nice way. This nice way may get her into serious trouble, especially if he misinterprets her wanting to "cool off" as wanting to go outside to be more intimate. She needs to learn to reject the behavior, not the person. A more honest and assertive response to the situation would be, "Yes, I am uncomfortable with the way you are kissing my neck, but I would like to keep on dancing if you'll stop it."

Take the example of a woman who is clearly upset, and a man in her life asks what is wrong. She answers, "Nothing!" but her body language more accurately reflects her feelings than do her words. She may mean that she is so upset she can't talk about it, or perhaps he is the one who caused her to be upset and she will not give him the satisfaction of knowing it. The message he receives is that maybe he can trust her body language, but not her words.

Men often do the same thing. If a man is upset, punching walls or crying, and an important woman in his life asks what is wrong, his response is likely to be "Nothing!" But he doesn't really mean nothing. He is likely to feel that he is not supposed to express emotion by crying; that if he talks about the problem he may start to cry. So he doesn't admit that there is a problem. The woman also learns that his words are not as reliable as his body language.

If men and women continue to say one thing in words and another with body language, their partners will not rely on words to understand what is really going on. It would be far more effective for us to be honest about our feelings; we would be much more likely to get what we really want without relying on our partners to guess.

Give Clear Messages

It's not possible to tell your partner what you want sexually if you don't know yourself. You receive many conflicting messages in your life about sex. Your parents probably tell you something different from the males your age, and that message is probably different from what you hear from your female peers, from the media, and from your religion.

These messages may be confusing, and to make matters worse your heart, your head, and your genitals may all be giving you conflicting messages. It is very important that you think about what you want sexually, sort out the conflicts, and try to communicate your conclusion clearly to your partner before both of you are feeling the urgency of sexual arousal or the relaxation of inhibitions that accompanies alcohol consumption.

When you have decided what you want sexually, you must communicate that clearly, giving the same message with your words and your body language. If you really don't want to have sex with him, don't tell him that you just want to be friends while you let him unbutton your blouse. Don't tell him that you don't want to have sex because you don't have any means of birth control; he may have a condom (rubber) in his wallet. If you don't want to have sex, make that clear with time parameters, such as, "I don't go to bed on the first date," or "I want to wait until marriage." If you say, "I don't want to have sex right now," he may think that five minutes later will be all right.

Avoid Dangerous Situations

The best way to avoid acquaintance rape is to keep out of situations that could become dangerous. It is not always easy to know which situations will be safe and which will not, but some general rules may help. Because they are general rules, it is important to remember that not all the situations described will actually be dangerous, and some that are not mentioned may be dangerous. Factors that are often associated with acquaintance rape include:

- alcohol and drug use;
- being isolated with a man;
- being with a man in a place where he is under a great deal of peer pressure;
- being with a man who exploits or ignores you;
- being with a man who exhibits antisocial behavior;
- not having your own transportation;
- feeling that your personal space is being violated.

The degree of intoxication of a man is the one most important factor in determining whether acquaintance rape will occur. Don't stay with a man who is drunk. If you yourself are intoxicated you will be less able to assess your situation and less effective in making your wishes known.

Being isolated with a man will eliminate the possibility of getting help. There may be no one to hear you if you call out. In addition, he may assume that your going with him to an isolated place means that you want to be intimate sexually. If he thinks that is what you intended, he may try to push you to have sex "for your own sake."

Some men who are kind and considerate when they are alone with a woman are coerced into doing unacceptable things when they are with others who pressure them. This factor is important in gang rape. Imagine a situation in which a group of fraternity men are trying to top each other's male prowess. They see who can drink more, who can lift more weights, and who can pick up women most quickly. If they are really drunk they may even discuss who has had sex with the most women. If a woman at a party is considered promiscuous, and she is also drunk, they may try to prove who is the "best man" by having sex with her. Some of the brothers may not want to participate but fear being made fun of or labeled gay or impotent. They may simply fear not being considered "one of the boys." Under these circumstances, an otherwise nice man may participate in gang rape.

Men who exploit others in nonsexual situations are more likely to exploit women in sexual situations. If you know someone who asks you to clean his room (just because you are a female), or who leaves you alone at a party where he knows many of the people and you know few, be careful around him in sexual situations. Such men believe that women are less valuable than men and that it is acceptable to treat them as sex objects. He may be the type who strikes a woman when he is angry or who thinks that a woman should meet his sexual desires regardless of her own.

Men who behave antisocially in nonsexual situations are also likely to force women to have sex. For example, men who drive drunk or break other laws are behaving in antisocial ways. Such people frequently do not exhibit regard for others in sexual situations either. If they want sex and their partner does not, they are likely to force sex.

If you do not have your own transportation home from a party or game, you are dependent on your date. If he should start to exhibit signs that you consider dangerous, it is important that you be able to leave without relying on him. Take money to call your parents or for bus or cab fare, or go with a friend who will be willing to drive you when you want to leave.

One of the earliest signs that a situation is becoming dangerous is for a man to invade your personal space and not back off when you tell him he is too close. Personal space is the imaginary boundary that surrounds each of us, the distance from another person we need to make us feel safe and comfortable. At a party, for example, a man starts to handle your necklace. This makes you uncomfortable, and you take the necklace out of his hand and back up. Your discomfort tells you he is too close.

If a stranger comes into an almost empty movie theater and sits in the seat next to you, that is an invasion of your personal space. The boundary varies with different people. A friend sitting next to you would not make you uncomfortable, your mother can come very close without your feeling violated, but your school principal must stay further away for you to feel comfortable.

Early in a relationship you have a wider personal space than you do after you have been dating for a year. If a date begins to violate your personal space, you must let him know that this is unacceptable. If he continues to stay too close, it is a sure sign that he is not taking your wishes into account. This is the universal first stage of acquaintance rape.

Have a Way Out

What can you do if you are in your own home with a man who you feel may try to force you to have sex? Walk out and leave him there if you sense danger and he won't leave. Go to a safe place, like a neighbor's home, where you can call the police to have him removed.

But what if you fear he won't let you leave through the front door? You should have an escape plan, another way out, like the back door or a window. Most acquaintance rapes take place in the victim's or the assailant's home. If he means to rape you and you leave, he may get angry and "trash" your house, but that is preferable to being raped. After all, the items in your home are replaceable. Your mental health is not so easily restored.

KNOW HOW TO USE YOUR WEAPONS

Your Mind

You can use your mind, your voice, or your body as a weapon. The first way to use your mind is to assess the potential danger level of a situation and avoid involvement. The second is to get out of a situation that has become frightening. The third is to get out of a situation in which you are in imminent danger.

In the first type of situation you use your mind to assess the potential danger. Imagine that David, a macho man whom you don't know well, suggests that you ride with him instead of on the bus provided for a ski trip. David has a reputation for being "fast." Your instincts tell you that many hours in a car with him would put you in a vulnerable situation. You would have virtually no control over events because he is much stronger than you are. If you decide not to go with him but to ride on the ski bus, you have probably made a wise decision. Even though you are attracted to him, you will have ample opportunity to get to know him better on the slopes, where many other people are around.

Suppose you are at a fraternity party and a friend introduces you to Tony, a delightful man whom you are enjoying. You dance for most of the evening. When things begin to slow down, he invites you to his room to see his new stereo. In his room you start to kiss and fool around, but at times he tries to push you further than you want to go sexually. He is pretty drunk and is honoring your protests less and less, and you are becoming increasingly uneasy. Just then someone knocks at the door asking to borrow one of his tapes. At that point you say, "It is getting late and I really must be getting home," and you leave the room while someone else is there for protection.

Your Voice

In both of those situations you used your mind to assess the potential for danger and made a decision to get out of the situation before anything dangerous actually happened. But what if you do not assess the situation as dangerous and you find that you are being forced to do something you don't want to do sexually? What if you cannot just leave to avoid the danger? How can you use your voice as a weapon? Many women feel embarrassed to raise their voice or scream because they have been taught that it is not ladylike. It is hard to confront someone directly and demand your rights, especially if you are with someone you like and with whom you want to develop a relationship.

The principles you must apply in such situations are these:

- It is better to be embarrassed than raped.
- Yelling may seem unladylike, but it may keep you safe.
- When women yell, men are more likely to take them seriously.
- Yelling when there is no one around to hear you is less effective than yelling where others can hear you.

Imagine being on a picnic in a quiet park with Kevin, whom you have dated just a few times. You are enjoying the afternoon sun, nature, and each other's company. Just when you thought things were going well, he begins to get very insistent about having sex "in a natural setting." You tell him that you don't want to have sex with him in any setting, but he doesn't seem to care. Finally in desperation you yell, "I don't want to have sex with you; if you force me, it is rape." He is likely to stop because he doesn't think of himself as a rapist. If he doesn't stop, however, it may be because he doesn't think you will tell anyone and no one else is around to hear you yell. Thus yelling may stop him because you startled him by what you said and how you said it; on the other hand it may not work because you are in a secluded place and no one will hear you yell.

Suppose your employer calls you into his office and starts to make sexual advances. You have heard that he has done this with other people, and you don't want to have sex with him. There are people in the outer office who will hear if you scream. He doesn't stop when you tell him to, so you yell, "Leave me alone, I don't want this." He does stop then because he fears what the others outside may think, but you are worried about his firing you because you wouldn't have sex with him. If he fires you for that reason, he has broken the law. You could take him to court for sexual harassment and unlawful dismissal. However, you may just decide that no job is worth having to deal with sexual coercion and be happy to be out of it. In either case, you used your voice effectively as a weapon.

Your Body

In the event that neither of the previous strategies works you may need to use a physical self-defense maneuver to get to a safe place. Self-defense is difficult for some women to learn because it is contrary to much female socialization.

If you have been told all your life not to hurt others, and certainly not to hurt them physically, it may be hard for you to employ the technique if the need arises.

To be effective in employing self-defense, you need to know the vulnerable target areas on the body (such as eyes, knees, ribs, neck, nose, instep), your effective weapons against the body (such as fists, feet, elbows, head), and how to strike effective blows with those weapons. The best way to learn is to take a self-defense course, perferably one designed for women. Then you must practice the techniques consistently to be effective when necessary. A good book on the subject is *Fear or Freedom—A Woman's Options in Social Survival and Physical Defense* by Susan Smith.

Know About Rapists

The most important thing to know about rapists, especially those who commit date or acquaintance rape, is that they usually appear normal, just like "any other man." Although some would argue that any man who *could* rape has psychological problems, he may not *appear* to be psychologically ill. In other words, you can't tell by looking at someone or even by talking with him if he is a rapist. Those who rape come from all socioeconomic classes and may be found in any occupation. Contrary to sex-role conditioning, a woman can't expect every man she goes out with to want to protect her.

Many men who commit acquaintance rape do not plan rape; they plan sex. That is to say, they plan to have sex at the end of the date, and if the woman does not comply they push her. Many such men do not think that they have done anything wrong, much less raped anyone. If you ask him at the end of the date if what happened was rape, he will probably say no. In fact, he may even say that the woman was asking for sex by inviting him to her house or by dancing seductively. He may believe that he was doing her a favor by giving her what she wanted without her having to take the responsibility for initiating sex. He may say that he didn't want to have intercourse with her but thought she wanted it and so he obliged.

The more you know about rape and rape prevention, the more you can avoid becoming involved in such situations. You will also know the options if you or someone you know is raped. If you know the common emotional responses to rape, you may be better able to deal with them.

WAYS TO MAKE THINGS SAFER IN THE FUTURE

Rape is hard to deal with if you've been victimized. You will need emotional help from a strong support system to be able to cope with the emotional reactions that follow rape. You may also be able to help others who have been raped because you possess a special understanding about the subject. You can use that understanding in the aftermath of rape to help others.

Volunteer at a Rape Crisis Center

Although not all of the good volunteers at Rape Crisis Centers have been raped, if you have been a victim you possess a special understanding of rape. You may be very effective at helping others because you understand what they have been through.

Volunteering to help others will be effective only if you

have worked through the emotional turmoil surrounding your own rape. Once you have done that, the experience may be helpful in two ways. First, you will be helping others who need support and not blame. Second, you are likely to regain a sense of the power and control over your life that you used to feel.

Work to Change the Law

In most states acquaintance rape and date rape are illegal, although they do not often end in conviction in the criminal justice system. In some states, however, these acts are not actually violations of law because of flaws in the law. For example, in about half of the states women cannot charge their husbands with rape. Also wide discretion is allowed law enforcement officials to decide if a rape charge will stand up in court. If they are not sure of the evidence, they are not likely to proceed with the case.

Laws can be changed to eliminate this discretion so that if a rape victim wants to press charges she may do so. Some states are considering laws that would require investigation of every incident of acquaintance rape reported on a college campus. Other changes being considered in some states include establishing marital rape as a crime, creating gender-neutral laws allowing for either males or females to be victims or assailants, and assimilating rape law into assault law. The latter would eliminate the introduction of past sexual history, eliminate the marital rape exception, do away with the high age of consent, and reduce the penalties for rape, meaning that more assailants would be convicted if the potential sentence were shorter.

If you would like to see justice in acquaintance rape situations, you may be very effective in providing input to lawmakers to change the laws so they will more effectively reflect the needs of society today. You may do so by writing to them, visiting them, and voting against those who do not treat the issue with the seriousness it deserves.

Attempt to Prosecute Your Rapist

Since many rapists repeat the offense many times, it is possible that your assailant has raped others and will continue to do so. If you choose to prosecute your rapist and he is convicted, the world may be safer in several ways. First, he will not have access to women while he is in prison. Second, in prison he may have access to a treatment program for sex offenders. Third, just by prosecuting you make clear to him that what he did was wrong; you embarrass him and call his character into question.

Educate Others About Rape

The more people know about rape, the less likely they are to blame the victim. If an acquaintance rape is reported to them they will be better able to be supportive to the victim and help her through the trauma. In addition, they are likely to provide correct information regarding evidence collection and reporting procedures. For instance, they can inform the victim that she does not have to press charges or make a decision about going to court immediately, but that early reporting to the police will make her case stronger if she does decide to go to court. If she never goes to court, the information she provides to the police may tell them more about this rapist and his patterns of behavior.

Informing others about rape will help to dispel some of the rape myths. The better informed people are, the better jurors they will be if they have to serve in a rape case. If jurors better understand rape, they will probably bring in more convictions in acquaintance rape cases, possibly resulting in a decrease of incidence. If the court system gives the message that acquaintance rape will be punished, perhaps fewer men will commit the crime.

Work for Improvement of Services

If you have been through a medical or legal examination following rape, you may have been one of the lucky ones who had a good experience. But you may have had a very bad experience if the professionals working with you were not well trained, or if they believed the rape myths. You have special expertise that could be helpful to medical and law enforcement agencies to help them improve the services that are available to rape victims.

Medical personnel should be trained in the use of the rape kit used to collect medical evidence. In addition, medical facilities should have a rape team of sensitive professionals who have streamlined the procedures so that the victim does not have to retell the details of the rape many times. Members of the rape team should include a female (if possible) physician, nurse practitioner, or physician assistant to collect the evidence (a male may seem threatening to the victim); a nurse, a social worker, a Rape Crisis Center volunteer, and a well-trained police officer. Each of these people has a specific job to do; they are all important to the team. A special private place should be available for the victim to wait in the hospital, rather than in the middle of the busy waiting area of the emergency room.

Police agencies should train staff members about acquaintance rape and also provide a private place for questioning in the police station. It is very difficult for a victim to recount the graphic details of the rape with a lot of people listening.

Work to Change Policies at Your School

If you are at a college, university, or boarding high school, the institution probably has policies to deal with violations of the law or of acceptable social behavior. If the administrators or campus police are not educated about acquaintance rape, they may fail to treat it as a crime; instead, they may blame the victim. Therefore it is important that they understand the crime and its consequences.

When a woman has been a victim of acquaintance rape, she frequently doesn't want to see the assailant again. If they go to the same school they will probably see each other on campus, which can be devastating for the victim. She often chooses to leave the school rather than have to see him daily. The institution should act swiftly in these cases to protect her psychological well-being; she should be given the choice of who is to be moved.

A judicial hearing should be held as soon as possible. It should be a private rather than a public hearing because many women faced with having to describe the attack in public refuse to testify. A timely hearing is also in the man's best interest; if he is found not guilty his name is cleared. The institution also needs to make counseling services available to both victim and assailant.

Help Develop Community Programs

The best thing you can do for others is to help them avoid rape. This may be accomplished through community education programs. Effective rape prevention programs frequently have a self-defense component.

You have information and knowledge about rape that many other people don't have, but you probably don't feel equipped to conduct rape awareness and prevention programs yourself. You may find supportive helpers in Rape Crisis Centers, the YWCA or YMCA, among local martial arts instructors, at counseling centers, in police agencies, hospitals, women's centers, colleges, universities, and men's groups. You may be helpful in a number of ways, depending on your skill level, but perhaps your most important role would be as an adviser regarding what would have been helpful to you.

Conclusion

Many suggestions and strategies in this chapter have been offered to make your world safer from rape. Some of the suggestions may work for you, but others may seem impossible. Don't feel that you have to adopt or learn any of the strategies. However, the more you incorporate into your life, the better protected you will be.

Nevertheless, it is important not to think you are invulnerable to rape once you have incorporated some of these suggestions into your life. These are tools to make you *safer*, not absolutely safe. The most important thing you can do is never to let down your guard. The more aware you are in all situations, the more you increase your safety. The more risks you eliminate, the less you will have to worry in the future.

You may find that you can do only a few of these things now. That's all right too. You may find that you are ready to try more and more as time goes on. Keep updating your rape prevention strategies. You may want to read this chapter periodically to see what new strategies you want to try. The more you do these things, the more likely they are to become second nature. Eventually you won't even have to think about doing them; they will come naturally.

CHAPTER 9

Not Just for Females—Males as Victims

Rape is not only a female problem. Males are involved in rape in many ways. The most obvious way is as assailants, and in fact most rapes are committed by men. But males as children and adults are also victims of sexual assault. Some men who sexually assault others were themselves victims of sexual assault as children.

In his book *Men Who Rape*, Nicholas Groth writes that the two most important aspects of manhood are strength and sexuality and when a man has been raped he has lost both or may feel that he has. In addition, men may be the fathers, lovers, brothers, or friends of rape victims. Men may be linked in many ways to rape.

Rape is not something men talk about very much, perhaps because men are not comfortable talking about their feelings, and rape is a very emotional topic for most people. Men also rarely admit to themselves or each other that they could be victims of rape.

What If You Were Raped by a Woman?

This is an uncommon phenomenon that we seldom hear about, but any man, like any woman, can be the victim of sexual assault. Size, strength, personality, or sexual orientation do not necessarily determine who will be raped. Women can use coercion, force, or violence to get men to have sex against their will. Men sometimes have involuntary erections. Almost every young man has experienced the problem around the beginning of puberty when his hormones were surging. The male hormone testosterone is associated with aggression and sexual drive. High levels of testosterone contribute to erections. So when teenage males have testosterone surges they often experience erections that they don't want and can't control.

When older men act aggressively or when their testosterone level is high they may also have uncontrollable erections. Some men experience erections they can't control when they are angry, afraid, or anxious. If a man is with a woman who wants to have sex and threatens him, he may have an erection.

Self-consciousness is the most common cause of impotence. Because of adrenaline (a hormone released in dangerous situations), the fear response often overpowers self-consciousness, allowing the erection mechanism to work. But an erection is not necessary for a man to become a victim of sexual assault. A man can be sodomized (forced to have oral or anal sex) against his will without having an erection.

ERIC

Eric was not very popular on campus and was embarrassed by his lack of friends. He desperately wanted to make friends but didn't know how to go about it. One day in psychology his lab partner Maria asked him if he would like to join a study group. He was delighted because he thought it would be a good opportunity to get to know some other people and perhaps develop a long-term friendship with Maria.

Maria invited Eric to her house that evening for a study session. When he arrived, four classmates were busily talking about social things. Eric wanted to join in but couldn't think of anything pertinent to add. He was feeling more socially inept than ever. Things got better once they started to discuss psychology because Eric had a better grasp of the material than the others.

Eric continued to feel uncomfortable and socially inept, but at a session a few weeks after he joined the group Maria asked him to stay afterwards to help her with a paper. Eric was nervous because he had never been very good with women, but he stayed anyway. After a while she started nuzzling up to him, which made him very uncomfortable, but he didn't know how to make her stop. He decided the best thing to do was to leave, but Maria began to fondle him and kiss him when he said he had to go.

She asked, "What's the matter, don't you like me?" He said he did but he had homework to do. He was very uncomfortable because he was a virgin. He didn't know what to do sexually, nor did he want to have sex with someone he didn't care about. Maria started to tease him and said there had been rumors in class that he was gay. If he didn't have sex with her she would know they were true.

Eric was in a panic. He was afraid that if he left she would tell everyone he was gay. Then he would be rejected by his peers or perhaps even beaten up. He was also embarrassed to tell Maria that he was a virgin. He had sex with her unwillingly and felt devastated afterwards. She made fun of his awkwardness and difficulty with his erection. He felt used and dirty, but he did not know whom to talk to, or even what to say.

He was sure that if he told any man on campus that Maria had forced him to have sex the response would be, "You lucky guy, I'd give anything to have sex with her. There must be something wrong with you if you had to be forced!" He didn't even know what to call what had happened. He thought rape was something that only happened to women, with male assailants, and that it usually involved force and violence.

Eric didn't tell anyone. He just tried to deal with his emotions himself. But it was a long time before he was able to function well in his school work or his personal life.

Maria used coercion to get Eric to comply, but women can use other ways to get men to have sex against their will. Women can use weapons or the threat of weapons. A woman who has power over a man can threaten abuse of that power; for example, a professor might threaten a failing grade, or a stepmother might withhold an allowance unless the male has sex.

This kind of sexual assault happens much less frequently than men forcing women, which makes it even harder for a male victim to talk about his problem. He may think he is the only one who has had the experience and that no one else will understand. Trained counselors know about these types of situations and can help. More information about where to go for help is given in Chapter VI.

What If You Were Sexually Assaulted by a Man?

Men are sometimes forced to have sex with other men. Many people mistakenly think that this proves that the rapist and the victim are homosexual. In reality, just as in the case of women victims, rape of men is usually motivated by a desire to dominate someone weaker or a compulsion to replay childhood experiences of sexual abuse. Many people think that a man who can be forced to have sex with another man must be unmanly, weak, gay, or all three and that a "real man" would fight the rapist off. This may not be possible if the rapist overpowers you or has a weapon. It is especially difficult if there is more than one assailant.

Most rapes of men by other men take place in prison. Men who rape men would probably choose women as victims if they were available. Since women are not available, they choose men whom they can dominate, manipulate, and degrade. If you asked the rapists of men if they considered themselves homosexual, most would say no.

Some men who have been raped by other men believe that such an act is sexual and must imply something about the sexuality of the victim. The person who was raped may think that something about him attracted the rapist and therefore he may have homosexual tendencies.

In fact something probably did draw the rapist to the victim, but it had nothing to do with sexual orientation. Rapists seek people they can dominate. If the victim appeared unsure of himself, lonely, or unhappy, the rapist may have assessed him as someone who wouldn't put up much of a fight.

Being raped by someone of your own sex does not mean anything about your sexual orientation. It is important to understand that rape is primarily an act of violence and only incidentally sexual. If someone beats you in the process of stealing your car, you are a victim of a violent crime. In the same way, if you are the victim of sexual assault by a man, it doesn't make you any more or less homosexual or heterosexual. It means you are the victim of a crime, not a willing sex partner. You may, however, feel less like having sex with anyone after the assault, because any activity involving the genitals is associated with the devastating experience of loss of control. Gradually, as you work through that feeling and feel more in control again, sex will be more appealing.

Responses to Sexual Assault

Men who have been sexually assaulted report feeling ashamed of not having avoided the attack or of being involved in a "perverse" sexual act. They often feel dirty and that their masculinity has been compromised. They may feel degraded or disgusted and question their sexual orientation and their masculinity.

Rape victims, whether male or female, need emotional help to deal with what happened to them and to help them regain a more healthy behavior pattern. Most Rape Crisis Centers have male and female counselors trained to help you with the emotions you experience after rape or sexual assault. Also a supportive and understanding friend or family member may be able to help you sort things out. There may be other professionals in your community who can help. Selecting the best support people is described in Chapter VI.

Men who have been victims of sexual assault often have trouble with their sexuality, or they may have sex with as many women as possible to prove to themselves that they are "normal." If they fear that they are gay, they may try to avoid any sexual feelings for fear of being aroused by other men. The fact is that one sexual encounter (voluntary or forced) with another man does not make you gay. Sexual orientation is determined in early life, and one act later in life will not change that.

Reporting

Studies show that men are much more likely to report rape if they tried to fight back, perhaps because they are less likely to be blamed if there is evidence of a fight. Many men won't accept counseling, considering it unmanly and an admission of helplessness. On the contrary, a trained counselor can help you regain your sex drive and feelings of power and self-esteem. If it will help you regain your strength and your sex drive, what could be more masculine?

CHAPTER 10

Why Do Nice Men Force Friends to Have Sex?

There are different types of sexual sharing. Sex when both partners are willing is called *consensual sex*. Sex when one person agrees to gratify the other person but will not receive pleasure in the act is called *altruistic sex*. In *complaint sex*, one partner complains that he or she does not want sex but the other continues until satisfied (most acquaintance rape falls into this category). The last category is *rape*, where sex is clearly forced or violence or coercion is used. Acquaintance rape may be either complaint sex or rape.

If you know someone who has raped and you don't do anything about it or you condone it, you are condoning rape in general. Taken one step further, sexist jokes (in which women are dehumanized or degraded) and violence toward women are forms of behavior that make rape seem more acceptable to men who may have the tendency to rape. It is hard to condemn sexist or pro-rape attitudes in groups where those attitudes are the norm. Unfortunately, when men get together they often make sexist jokes or discuss women as objects.

Most people do not know the legal definition of rape, nor do they know exactly what constitutes rape. Many men assume that they have never raped because they think rape is a violent act committed by a stranger. By learning the definition and discussing what behaviors constitute rape, many men might have to face the fact that they have forced a woman to do something sexual against her will. In other words, they may have raped.

What If You Committed Rape?

Many men who commit acquaintance or date rape do not know they have committed a crime. Remember, the definition of rape is forcing a woman to have intercourse without her consent or if she is fearful for her life or afraid of injury. She is not able to consent if she is unconscious, asleep, under seventeen years of age (in most states), or mentally incompetent. If you forced, threatened, used violence, or coerced a woman to have sex under any of those circumstances, it was rape if intercourse occurred or sexual assault if other sexual acts occurred.

Men tend to assign a sexual meaning to certain behaviors that women would consider friendly. For example, if a woman invites a man to her apartment for a Pepsi after a date she may merely want to be friendly. Her date may assume that is it meant as a sexual come-on and think he has "a right" to force her to have sex. Therefore, she will have to put up active resistance because he assigned his own meaning to her behavior.

Men often blame women for causing rape. Psychiatric views have even included blaming an overbearing or "cold" mother. "Frigid" wives or "provocative" victims have also been blamed. These ideas ignore the fact that the man has free will. He can choose to rape or not rape.

In other situations mental illness, alcoholism, or uncontrollable impulse have been cited as reasons for rape. In most cases, especially acquaintance rape, the assailant has no clear signs of mental illness. He is able to control his other impulses in life, and if he does not, he is held accountable for them. For example, if he has an impulse to shoot a neighbor's dog he would be arrested, not excused because he couldn't control himself, or because he'd been drinking, or because he was mentally ill.

Alcohol is often involved in acquaintance rape situations, but it doesn't justify rape. Some people excuse a man for forcing a woman to have sex when he was drunk because "he couldn't help himself," as though he were like a runaway train that can't be stopped. Men are held accountable for committing other crimes while drunk, and the same standards are applicable in rape situations. The law doesn't consider drunkenness a defense.

Finally, men have been excused from the charge of rape because of "victim precipitation," which means that the victim caused the rape. In no other situation do we dismiss a crime because of the *victim's* behavior. For example, if a man walks in a bad part of town and is mugged, we do not excuse the crime because he shouldn't have been there. But in acquaintance rape the assailant is all too often excused if the victim went to his apartment willingly.

In a survey of high school students, researchers found that males were more likely than females to think a non-verbal action had a sexual meaning. More than one third of the males thought it was acceptable to force a woman to have sex if she had "led him on," if he had spent a lot of money on her, if he knew she had had sexual intercourse with other men, if he was "so turned on he couldn't stop," if she was intoxicated, if she let him touch her above the waist, and if they had been dating a long time. More than half thought that forced sex was acceptable if she changed her mind; that is, first said yes and then decided she didn't want it. But women are never responsible for being victims of rape. The person who forces sex is the one who is responsible for the rape. None of the above conditions are acceptable moral, ethical, or legal explanations for forcing someone to have sex.

Some men justify forced sex if a woman was drinking and passed out, saying that she was asking for it. This is not true according to the law. And if one thinks about the situation, it's hard to imagine how one can ask for something when unconscious.

Some men fall back on the fiction that a woman never really means no in a sexual situation. But if a woman did say no and did mean it and she is then forced to have sex, she was raped. Still others maintain that if a woman has had consensual sex with a man in the past he "has a right" to sex with her again. The law makes no reference to previous sexual experiences with the victim; previous acts, consensual or forced, are irrelevant.

Some people believe the myth that rape happens only when a stranger jumps out of the bushes and beats a woman in the process of forcing her to have sex. In fact, rape without obvious violence by an assailant who knows the victim occurs much more often than stranger rape.

JOHN

Sue was a very sexy-looking young woman whom John met at a party. He had been hearing about her for weeks from his buddies on the hockey team, who said

she was "loose" and interested in many sexual prac-
tices. Sue was a real hockey fan and went to all the
games. After one game when John made a game-
winning goal, Sue called to say that she was very im-
pressed and would like to help him celebrate. Was he
available to go to a party with her next Friday night?
John said yes and hurried to tell his buddies about his
date. They immediately started telling him about all
the sexual activities he had to look forward to with
Sue.

When Friday finally came he picked Sue up and
they went to the party. She drank a lot and danced
very seductively. At the end of the party she invited
John to her house for something to drink and said her
roommates were out of town for the weekend.

They were both pretty drunk when they got there,
but they continued drinking. John started to kiss and
undress her, and Sue seemed to be enjoying it. When
he tried to take her pants off, she told him no, but he
thought she was being coy. Besides he had heard that
she was into S & M (kinky forced sex). He continued
to try to undress her and she fought harder. John
couldn't understand why she would want to be forced,
but he was willing to oblige.

He finally succeeded in having intercourse with her
after a half hour of struggle. She stopped resisting
when he was kneeling on her legs and holding her
arms down. The next day in the locker room he
proudly reported the events of the previous evening
to his teammates.

John thought the date was great, but Sue was raped. In
reality, she usually refused sex, and because of that a few
angry and rejected dates had started rumors about her.

John believed that she had had sex with everyone else and assumed that she would want him too. He believed that the messages she gave proved that she was a loose young woman: She called him up for the date, she drank a lot, she danced suggestively, she invited him to her house, and she told him her roommates were away for the weekend. John wanted sex and he wanted to believe that she wanted it too, so he decided that no must be part of a sexual game she was playing. Since he was drunk he was not able to assess the situation correctly.

John may never know that he raped Sue. If he does find out he may deny it, or he may feel terrible because he believes himself to be a kind and moral person.

What Are Your Feelings?

After reading this chapter, if you believe you may have forced someone to have sex you may be feeling bad about having committed rape. You may need to talk to a counselor to help you understand what actually happened and how you should change your behavior to avoid raping again. You may want to think about how to interact with your partner in the future. Some communities have men's discussion groups that deal with these kinds of issues. You may also find helpful the book *Men on Rape* by Timothy Beneke.

How Can You Help to Avoid Rape?

If you think you may have committed acquaintance rape and you want to make sure you don't do it again, there are several things you can do. You can work toward changing your behavior. You can also have a significant impact if you talk to other men about the issue and help them learn ways to change their behavior, and the importance of doing so.

Use Peer Pressure in a Positive Way

Men often use peer pressure to reinforce negative behaviors regarding women and sex. For example, men ask each other, "How far did you get last night?" That kind of question puts pressure on the man to make sure he has something to report to his buddies, regardless of the woman's wishes. If he didn't have sex with her, he may lie about it, thereby giving her a "bad reputation." When other men go out with her they will expect the same treatment as their buddy reported, whether it was true or not. So the woman may be forced to have sex by a second man because he believes she had sex with the first man and he is angry that she says no to him.

Rather than asking a friend how far he got after a date, you can ask him if he enjoyed her company and if they liked the movie. Think of the young woman as a person rather than a sex object, and encourage your friends to do the same.

If you hear your friends talking about a woman as a sex object, tell them you don't like to hear women put down and try to help them understand the problem with such behavior. Be sure to give them suggestions of alternative ways of discussing these issues.

Try to Meet Your Need for Intimacy Through Other Men

One reason men feel they need to have sex so often is that our society does not offer them many other options to fulfill their need for intimacy. If men could be more comfortable having emotionally close friends, they would not need to turn to sex to substitute physical closeness for emotional closeness. Unfortunately this kind of behavior is not encouraged. Men are often afraid to share their feelings for fear of being thought weak or unmanly. Whether they talk about them or not, almost all men have feelings of pain, insecurity, and rejection. Sharing those feelings with other men can help a man discover that he is not alone and that the feelings are normal. Most communities have men's groups that advocate developing close emotional relationships between men.

Some men are afraid to develop close emotional relationships because they associate emotional closeness between men with homosexuality. Although some homosexual men have relationships that are emotionally close, not all do. Conversely, heterosexual men can also have very close emotional relationships with other men. Emotional sharing does not necessitate sexual sharing, nor does a man's sharing emotions mean that he is a sissy or gay. It does, however, expand his options of human interaction and will probably keep him healthier in the long run because supportive relationships reduce stress.

Understand That Sex Is Not Emotional Intimacy

Many people assume that sexual intercourse automatically involves emotional intimacy. The two may go hand in hand but often do not. Think of the people to whom you feel closest: perhaps your mother, brother, a teammate, a teacher, your best friend. What is it about those relationships that causes you to feel close? Sex is probably not the reason. There are other factors that foster emotional intimacy, like sharing feelings, discussing important events and moments, and helping each other during difficult times.

Many people have one-time sexual encounters, "one-night stands." They know very little about the person they

have sex with. Sex itself does not make an encounter emotionally intimate. They may have shared physical intimacy
but no emotional intimacy at all. If what you need is an
emotionally intimate relationship, you need to share feelings and experiences, not simply sex. Sexual encounters
that have no emotional component are likely to leave
you disappointed and feeling empty if you were in need of
emotional intimacy.

Respect Your Partner

Many acquaintance rapes occur because the man thinks he
has more of a right to his desires than does his partner. This
usually happens if he believes he is "better" than his
partner. One way to avoid acquaintance rape is to date only
women who you think are equal to you. If you can't find
such dates, perhaps you should reconsider what it is that
makes someone important and valuable to you. Perhaps
your priorities need to be redefined.

Listen to the Messages Your Partner Gives

People can give messages in two ways, verbal and
nonverbal (body language). We often rely on body language to know what a person really means, but unfortunately we do not always interpret the message correctly. In
a sexual situation, for example, a woman's no may be interpreted as no, maybe, or yes. How does a man interpret the
word if he doesn't believe she means what she says? Is it
her inflection, her accompanying hand gestures, her tone
of voice, what she does with her body, her past behavior,
or a combination of several of these. If you read the cues
wrong, you may make the wrong judgment. Most of us are
not good mind readers when we want something so much

that it clouds our ability to understand that our partner does not want the same thing.

Suppose you base your decision on past behavior and believe that no means yes, but this time she really means no. Perhaps something is different about her situation today; she does not feel well, she is worried about not having a means of birth control, or she just isn't in the mood. Just because no meant yes in the past does not mean it ever will again.

Suppose she giggles when she says no and you take that to mean that she is not serious. Perhaps her giggle means that she is ticklish, or uncomfortable about what you are doing. You can't assume that anything you believe to be inconsistent body and verbal language gives you the green light.

A better way to handle the situation would be to stop what you are doing the first time she says no. If she really meant no she will be delighted that you stopped. If she meant maybe or yes, she will wonder what you are doing. She may say, "Why did you stop?" and you can respond, "Because you said no." If she says she didn't really mean no, she will have to take the responsibility if she wants to continue. An advantage of that is that you will not be in the usual position of facing possible rejection. If she is the one to initiate, she will be the one facing rejection. In addition, you will never have to wonder if you have forced someone to do something she didn't want to do. And you won't face the possibility of a police officer showing up at your home to arrest you for committing a rape that you didn't think you committed.

You can also be honest and direct by asking a woman if she would like to go to bed with you, if that if your intention. Consider something like, "Why don't we go to my apartment where we can be alone and go to bed if we both agree?"

You Too Can "Have a Headache"

One reason men force women to have sex is that many men feel pressured to be always ready and willing to have sex. A man may think, "No matter what the circumstances, the evening has to end in a sexual encounter or I have failed." He feels forced to be what he thinks is "normal." Being normal means doing what feels right for you. If you don't feel like having sex with every woman you go out with, you should feel free to say no.

Understand the Law

Not knowing that what you did was wrong won't save you from having to deal with the criminal justice system. If you break the law, you are likely to have to pay the consequences. Acquaintance and date rape are against the law. Men who commit acquaintance rape are frequently surprised that they have been arrested and indicted for a serious crime. The long-term consequences of a felony conviction are serving time in prison, having a criminal record, and losing your reputation. If you are arrested but not indicted, others may still know that you have been suspected of the crime and may view you differently. It could also hurt you chances for a job if the application asks whether you have ever been arrested.

Conclusion

Acquaintance rape and sexual assault are crimes that touch men as important people in the lives of the victims, as victims themselves, or as assailants. It is important for men to learn as much as possible about rape and sexual assault prevention. Following are important points that all men should know:

1. Rape is a crime of violence motivated by the desire to control and dominate.
2. It is never acceptable to force yourself on a woman even if you think she has been leading you on or you have heard that women say no but mean yes.
3. When you use force to have sex, you are committing a crime even if you know the woman or have had sex with her before.
4. You don't always have to initiate sex; you can say no too.
5. Whenever a partner says no—stop! Otherwise you may be committing rape.
6. The best way to avoid rape is to have a clear, honest discussion of whether your partner wants sexual intimacy and whether you both are protected against pregnancy and sexually transmissible diseases.

Appendix

RESOURCES

Where can you go for help in your community? There are a number of different kinds of places, depending on where you live. Follow these suggestions to reach someone who can help you decide what to do.

Rape Crisis Centers

1. Look up "Rape" in the phone book.
2. Call the operator and say that you have been raped and you want to be connected with the Rape Crisis number.
3. Call the YWCA and ask for the nearest Rape Crisis Center.
4. Call a suicide prevention hotline in your area.
5. Contact your school's counseling center or health center.
6. Call the police and ask for the number of a rape counseling center or a specially trained officer who deals with rape.
7. Call the Anti Social and Violent Behavior Center at (301) 443-3728 for a directory of Rape Crisis Centers and hotlines, or write to:

   Pennsylvania Coalition Against Rape
   2200 N. 3rd Street
   Harrisburg, PA 17110
   (717) 232-6745

8. Write to the National Coalition Against Sexual Assault (NCASA) to find out the location of the nearest center.

For Connecticut, Maine, Massachusetts, New Hampshire, New Jersey, New York, Pennsylvania, Rhode Island, or Vermont, write to:

NCASA: Robin Page   (617) 791-9546
Rape Crisis Program of Worcester
1016 Main Street
Worcester, MA 01603

For District of Columbia, Kentucky, Maryland, North Carolina, South Carolina, Tennessee, Virginia, West Virginia, or Delaware, write to:

NCASA: Ginny Welch   (615) 352-1716
Tennessee Coalition Against Sexual Assault
5716 Vino Ridge Drive
Nashville, TN 37205

For Iowa, Illinois, Indiana, Kansas, Michigan, Minnesota, North Dakota, South Dakota, Nebraska, Ohio, or Wisconsin, write to:

NCASA: Heidi Kon   (312) 769-0205
Rape Victim Services
Edgewater Uptown Community Mental Health Center
4740 N. Clark Street
Chicago, IL 60640

For Alabama, Arkansas, Florida, Georgia, Louisiana, Mississippi, or Missouri, write to:

NCASA: Doris McFarland   (904) 257-6055
State Attorney's Office
440 S. Beach Street
Baytona Beach, FL 32014

For Alaska, Idaho, Montana, Oregon, Utah, Washington, or Wyoming, write to:

NCASA: Mary Theresa Li   (503) 775-0606
4031 South East Long
Portland, OR 97202

For Arizona, California, Colorado, Hawaii, Nevada, New Mexico, Oklahoma, Pacific Territories, or Texas, write to:

NCASA: Mary Loring   (303) 322-7010
Ending Violence Effectively
P.O. Box 18212
Denver, CO 80218

Victims' Assistance Programs

call the National Organization for Victim Assistance (NOVA) at (718) 232-8560.

Self-defense Programs

1. Look in the phone book under Karate, Judo, or Martial Arts.
2. Call your YWCA or YMCA.

Gay and Lesbian Services

1. Look in the phone book under Gay or Lesbian.
2. Contact the National Gay Task Force Hotline: in New York (212) 529-1604; all other states, (toll-free) (800) 529-1604.

Organization for Males

Men Stopping Rape, Box 305, 306 North Brooks Street, Madison, WI 53715. Phone: (608) 157–5718.

Glossary

acquaintance rape   Forced sexual intercourse (or other sexual act) between two people who know each other.

aggravated rape   Rape in which a weapon, threat, violence, or force is used.

aggression   Demanding one's wishes without regard for the rights of others.

anger rapist   Rapist who is angry at women in general or one woman in particular.

assertiveness   Asking for your wishes without violating the rights of others.

civil suit   Legal action in which a victim sues the assailant personally.

consensual sex   Sexual intercourse (or other sexual act) between two willing partners.

criminal prosecution   Legal action in which the State prosecutes a defandant.

crisis phase   Stage of the rape trauma syndrome that follows immediately after the rape.

date rape   Forced sexual intercourse (or other sexual act) that occurs between a dating couple or while on a date.

disorientation phase   Stage of the rape trauma syndrome in which the victim loses emotional balance and has trouble interacting with other people.

force   physical violence or threat of violence; coercion or threat of coercion.

heterosexual   Having sexual interest in persons of the opposite sex.

homosexual   Having sexual interest in persons of the same sex.

marital rape   Forced sexual intercourse (or other sexual act) between husband and wife.

message, nonverbal Body language that conveys a meaning different from the verbal message given.

myths, rape Common but erroneous beliefs about the crime of rape.

personification Referring to parts of the body by proper names.

power rapist Rapist whose drive is a need to exercise power over a helpless victim.

rape Forced sexual intercourse (or other sexual act) against the will of the victim.

Rape Shield laws Statues that bar revelation in court of a rape victim's previous sexual experience.

rape trauma syndrome Series of phases experienced by a victim of rape.

reorientation phase Stage in the rape trauma syndrome when the victim begins to regain control of her emotions and life.

sadistic rapist Rapist whose drive is to torture and mutilate his victim.

sexual assault Rape, particularly of a male victim.

sexual intercourse Penetration of the penis into the vagina.

simple rape Rape in which no violence, threat, or struggle occurs.

socialization Method by which children are taught their stereotypic sex roles.

soft rape Forced sexual intercourse (or other sexual act) in which coercion or threat of coercion is used to gain the victim's compliance.

stranger rape Premeditated rape by a person unknown to the victim.

virgin A person who has not had consensual sexual relations.

Bibliography

Bart, P. *Stopping Rape: Successful Survival Strategies.* New York: Pergamon Press, 1985.

Benedict, H. *Recovery: How to Survive Sexual Assault for Women, Men, Teenagers, Their Friends and Families.* Garden City, NY: Doubleday & Company, 1985.

Beneke, Timothy. *Men on Rape: What They Have to Say about Sexual Violence.* New York: St. Martin's Press, 1982.

Estrich, Susan. *Real Rape.* Cambridge: Harvard University Press, 1987.

Federal Bureau of Investigation. *Uniform Crime Reports.* Washington, DC: U.S. Government Printing Office, 1984.

Giarrusso, R., Johnson, P., Goodchilds, J., and Zellman, G. "Adolescents' Cues and Signals: Sex and Assault." Paper presented at the annual meeting of the Western Psychological Association, San Diego, California, April 1979.

Groth, Nicholas A. *Men Who Rape*: The Psychology of the Offenders. New York: Plenum Press, 1979.

Koss, M., and Harvey, M. *The Rape Victim: Clinical and Community Approaches to Treatment.* Lexington, MA: Stephen Greene Press, 1987.

Muehelenhard, C., and McFall, R. "Dating Initiation from a Woman's Perspective." *Behavior Therapy, 12,* 1981.

Pritchard, C. (1987). *Avoiding Rape On and Off Campus,* 2d ed. Wenonah, NJ: State College Publishing Company, 1987.

Rowland, Judith. (1985). *The Ultimate Violation–Rape Trauma Syndrome: An Answer for Victims, Justice in the Courtroom.* New York: Doubleday and Company, 1985.

Smith, Susan E. (1986). *Fear or Freedom: A Woman's Options in Social Survival and Physical Defense.* Racine, WI: Mother Courage Press, 1986.

Index